# Law of Life

**By Rose Marie**

To my dearest friend,
Lee
Lots of success
Rose Marie

ISBN: 978-1-963017-49-6 (paperback)

ISBN: 978-1-963017-63-2 (Hardcover)

Printed in the United States of America

*Dedicated to All the Dreamers in the World*

# Contents

# PART 1

*The only way to make sense out of change is to plunge into it, move with it, and join the dance. – Alan Watts*

# Chapter 1

With briefcase in hand, Grant Priestly, CEO of Priestly Enterprises, paused at his personal assistant's office. 'Laura, I'm leaving for the HMA meeting. I don't expect to be needed, but if something comes up that can't wait until tomorrow morning, text me.' As an afterthought, he added, 'I forgot to tell you, Adrian is leaving for Munich in about,' with a quick look at his watch, 'Actually, he left about an hour ago.'

Grant's PA barely acknowledged her boss as she glared at the four stacks of papers that had taken over her desk. Not pausing with her task, she began sorting through the documents for the third time, attempting to locate an elusive addendum that was required for the upcoming Annual General Meeting. Since Laura managed Grant's calendar, she knew the appointment times, including his monthly HMA meeting. Her mind was distracted as she tried to recall which pile in which she saw Addendum XIII. She knew it had been printed and thought it was in the fourth pile.

Grant's words barely registered in her subconsciousness as she automatically responded, 'No problem. Have a good meeting.' Mentally reviewing her boss' words, she stopped shuffling and looked up. 'Grant, did you say that Adrian is leaving for Munich today? I thought his conference was next week?'

Priestly Enterprises consisted of two divisions. The original division, which was the legal firm started by Grant's parents. As their legal business prospered, Russell Priestly was seeking additional office space for his increased business dealings when he realized the economic advantages of commercial property ownership in a rapidly expanding city. With this foresight, a second division was created for commercial property development.

Adrian King was the Legal Division's President. Rarely was Adrian involved with an individual legal case. However, this specific case had several unique aspects that required his International Human Rights expertise. The last-minute trip to Germany was known by only a few associates.

Grant filled in the missing information for Laura. 'About four hours ago, we found out that the conference which was set up for next week was changed to tomorrow. By accident, Fritz Munitz heard about the change and got the information to us. I'm sure we will receive a formal notification about the date change any minute,' he concluded sarcastically. 'Adrian should be in the air by now.'

Laura nodded her head in acknowledgment. 'Okay. I doubt if anyone will need you this afternoon. It has been a pretty quiet day.' Laura resumed her search for Addendum XIII. She looked up at her boss, 'See you tomorrow.'

'Don't stay too late.'

Laura had been with the company for nearly eight years. Fresh from receiving her master's degree in fine arts and thousands of dollars in debt, Laura originally took the position at Priestly's until she could find employment within her field. Her first position was as a clerk for five of the real estate attorneys. Initially, she found the role boring and routine. She reasoned since it included a slightly better-than-average paycheck, her goal was to remain at Priestlys for a year while organizing her next career move. Many of the other clerks were law students or recent law graduates. As they moved forward with their career paths, Laura remained as a clerk past her self-defined deadline. The ability to pick up new tasks quickly was recognized by her supervisors. Laura was well-liked by most of her co-workers, who appreciated her friendly, positive attitude. Less charitable co-workers sniped at her very obvious and stunning physical appearance. For whatever reasons, Laura received several opportunities to vary her workload. Instead of leaving, Laura was eventually promoted to one of the six administrative assistants for the father and son, Russell and Grant Priestly.

Laura was impressed with the variety of responsibilities within her new position. She quickly realized that Priestly Enterprises had almost nothing in common with the popular legal television programs that focused on attorneys, lawyers, and their oversexed staff. The longer she was employed by Priestlys, the more the legal drama shows developed into comedy entertainment for her.

For instance, when she was first hired, she equated lawyers and attorneys with the same idiom. When she said as much to one of her co-workers, she was snobbishly corrected. A lawyer is someone who has learned and trained in law, yet they may not be able to practice law. They generally gave law advice. An attorney-at-law (or an attorney) practices law in the courts after passing their bar exam.

Nearly five years ago, when Grant began assuming the majority of the CEO's tasks from his father, Laura was offered the opportunity to work as his senior administrator and personal assistant. Her new role included supervising four junior administrative staff. Despite the non-stop hectic pace, she rarely regretted the path her career had taken.

It must be immediately acknowledged that the relationship between Laura and Grant was strictly business. The office rumor mill continuously speculated if another, less business relationship was developing. The gossipers went into overdrive a year ago when Laura and her husband finalized their divorce. It was well known that Grant had been divorced for several years, and he was not romantically linked with anyone. Or was he? Would Grant and Laura become an item? They seemed so compatible in the office. Most people would understand if the next step included a romantic relationship. However, not even the most ardent scandalmonger could detect a romance. Despite the multiple social activities, which included Priestly Enterprises, Laura and

Grant never attended any functions as a couple. More surprisingly, there were no working late at the office.

One of the reasons why conversations continued to create romances between them was because they physically looked so good together. If Walt Disney wanted models for his latest movie hero and heroine, the drop-dead blonde gorgeousness of Laura, in addition to Grant's classical dark Mediterranean physique, could be his models. Instead of any better gossip, some co-workers discussed the imaginary children of Grant and Laura. Depending upon the person speaking, they may also speculate on how the illusory child was conceived. If Laura wore an outfit that did not hug her picturesque curves, conjunction about a potential baby bump would circulate.

Grant was continuously asked by his single and, at times, married friends to hook them up with Laura. On an equally consistent basis, Laura was asked about the desirability of Grant Priestly. Her routine response was, 'Good bosses and good jobs are harder to find than boyfriends.' Grant's even-temper persona was well known to his employees, especially when they compared him to his father. When Russell Priestly was actively in charge, his frequent tyrannical explosions were legendary to everyone from the mail room to the board room. In reality, Laura knew a lot less about Grant's social life than people thought. She enjoyed Grant's good qualities, but there were times when she found his personal life - dare she say it – boring.

Although Laura had introduced her current boyfriend to several people, some people refused to give up their Grant / Laura fantasy.

It was early afternoon as Grant made his way to the exit of the five-story corporate Priestly building. Taking the elevator to the first floor, Grant shared the ride with Hasfa Hassan, Priestly's marketing director. They discussed last-minute details regarding the upcoming AGM. Most of the four hundred employees had returned from their lunch, and it was too early for them for the day. As he walked to his car, Grant appreciated a few minutes of silence while casually observing the snow-covered parking lot. During the winter months in upper-state New York, most high-end automobile owners put their expensive cars into garages. Two years earlier, Grant purchased his Aston Martin DB11. He told his friends that the car was for investment purposes. The car featured a sleek, deep royal blue and aerodynamic design. The car was powered by a 5.2-liter V12 engine that produces 630 horsepower with a top speed of 208 mph which could go from 0 to 60 mph in just 3.6 seconds. The purchase did not fool anyone into thinking that Grant owned the car to get groceries at Wegmans Supermarkets.

In the morning newscast, the local weatherman predicted temperatures would be cold enough that when the snow shower ended, the white stuff would remain on the ground. As predicted, the snow had stopped a few hours earlier. The snowplows had cleared the greater part of the company's parking lot. Three medium-sized snow mountains sat on the edges as if to guard the employees' cars. Glancing upwards, Grant noticed a single patch of bright, cobalt blue sky. Seeing any type of blue skies was unusual in November when dismal steel gray was normal with no hint of sunshine. The air was brisk. No other word can describe the feeling, thought Grant as the snow crunched under each footstep. The stillness was broken by the sounds of heavy goods trucks speeding down a nearby highway. When the Priestlys decided to build their new corporate headquarters on the outskirts of Rochester, the local highway was included in the consideration since it made the headquarters easy to access for both clients and employees.

As his car sped down the highway into the city, Grant shifted his mental gears away from business issues. Doing a few rapid calculations regarding the flow of traffic at this time of day, which streets would have been plowed, and the amount of drive time to reach the Regency Hotel's Conference Center, Grant was confident that he would arrive in plenty of time. Once behind the wheel, the transition from Priestly Enterprises issues to issues faced by the HMA's Board of Directors began to unfold in mind.

As an officer of a significant-sized corporation, Grant found himself involved in a variety of community projects. Most of these organizations, he inherited from his father's time as CEO. Until a couple of years ago, Grant regarded participating in local charities as a component of Priestly Enterprise's business model. He gave what he considered his fair share of time and money until he was personally affected by an unforeseen tragedy.

Passing the nearby elementary school, Grant had a flashback image of an eight-year-old Jack with his mischievous, lopsided grin and spikey blonde hair, which always seemed to need a haircut. Once Grant began reminiscing about his friend, his mind followed a well-traveled path to when he and Jack first met while at St Mary's Elementary School.

For the majority of their school activities, the teaching Sisters of Saint Joseph lined up students by their surnames. Jack Peterson and Grant Priestly spent eight years standing rigidly together in alphabetical order. Within a short time of being thrown together, Jack and Grant became the dynamic duo. Jack would come up with outlandish schemes. Grant would devise methods on how to make them work. As they progressed from elementary school to high school, their friendship became stronger. Upon graduation from high school, Grant decided to immediately follow his parents' path into the legal field. Jack attempted to convince his best friend to take a gap year before college. Jack reasoned that, with their parents' wealth, they could travel to any place in the world and have an adventure or two before settling down. With strong suggestions from his father, Grant decided to give his gap year a miss.

Jack was enjoying his solitary gap year when he learned about Grant's beloved mother's tragic death. Without hesitation, Jack caught the next flight back from Cambodia. For the next twelve difficult months, Jack was not far from his friend. Many times, Jack pulled his friend back from the abyss of depression. Jack even enrolled at Cornell University, the same as Grant. Whereas Jack enjoyed the collegiate social functions in and around Ithaca, his scholastic work was so poor that failure was inevitable at the end of the year. The Peterson family convinced Jack it was time to start working within the family's automotive business. When the Petersons extended their vehicle dealership franchises into Connecticut, Jack moved to New London. Eventually, Jack did what was expected of him. In short order, he was married and became a father, not necessarily in that order. Grant was the best man at Jack's lavish society wedding.

Grant was at the hospital within hours after the birth of Jack and Marilyn's son and two years later for the birth of their twin daughters. Grant remarked to his nervous friend, 'Someone needs to bring the cigars.' Champagne was substituted since neither smoked. The nurse on duty objected to alcohol in the hospital. Since it was after midnight, Grant charmed the nurse into allowing them to use an unused consultation room to toast the newborn daughters. Despite the fact Jack and his family lived nearly 400 miles away, the friends would meet up every couple of months.

The economy began to slow down in 2005 and remained in the same state the following year. It was a difficult time for most people – the retail industry, consumers, and politicians who continue to make unfilled promises. Numerous businesses were affected. This was especially true for any business connected to the automotive industry. Among the many causalities were Peterson's automotive franchises. In an economy where people were being laid off at an alarming rate, many people decided to make their current vehicle last another year or two. Grant knew his friend's financial situation could not be good.

When Grant tried to talk to Jack about the family's business, he laughed away any concerns regarding the economy. Jack stated with his usual optimistic bluster that everything was under control. A year into the recession, Jack's father abruptly retired and moved to South Carolina. It was not known to Grant until much later that Jack committed the last of his family's resources in an attempt to maintain the remaining car franchises using a marginally legal accounting practice. He had borrowed against the almost non-existent corporate assets. When Jack's parents died within months of each other, Grant, who was preoccupied with his marriage in turmoil, did not recognize Jack's emotions were beyond the grief of a child for his parents. Besides, Grant internally reasoned, why didn't Jack turn to him if he needed assistance?

Grant's fingers tightened around the steering wheel as he remembered his lame excuses for not helping his best friend. Six years had passed, and he still cringed with guilt at his selfish memories. After everything Jack had done for him, why couldn't Jack talk to him? Why didn't he make more of an effort to talk to Jack? Whatever the underlying reasons, Jack and Marilyn divorced. Marilyn and the children moved closer to her parents in Monterey Park, California. Jack had refused to interact with any of his friends, even Grant. Grant gave Jack the space that Jack claimed he wanted. What made Grant even more disgusted with himself was the knowledge that he didn't work harder to find out what was happening to Jack. During that time, Grant did not recognize indicators of mental health issues.

Grant heard about Jack's death and funeral through an acquaintance. The knowledge that he was not available for his best friend was like a punch to the gut every time he thought about it. Jack died in a homeless shelter. Dead at thirty-nine. Why? All through life and after so many escapades, Jack seemed unbeatable. As he searched for answers to understand why and what happened to his Jack. Grant began examining more closely one of his token charities, the Housing Management Association (HMA). The HMA was one of the charities in which his father had minimal involvement.

Instead of finding just one answer to the circumstances that surrounded the later part of his friend's life, he learned that rarely, no single setback could be applied to people who found themselves homeless. Generally, it would start with some unexpected situation, such as losing a job. Then, several adverse conditions would layer themselves upon a person until they could not free themselves without external support. The core theme of the HMA was to identify the primary difficulties of its clients who found themselves without a residence. HMA attempted to function across multiple agencies, both governmental and non-government, and to assist in alleviating the conditions that were the result of addictions, abuse, and mental or financial issues. Like most cities, even if all the problems were managed, Rochester still had a severe lack of affordable housing.

Recently, HMA had developed two new programs. A program directed towards specific women's issues. The second program was addressing the escalating problem of homelessness amongst younger people. As Grant became involved with various programs, he was so repulsed with himself that he didn't work harder to find out what happened to Jack. Working with HMA, he realized that there were many

'Jacks' and 'Jills.' Regardless of the time and funds Grant donated to the HMA's cause, he couldn't fully resolve the pangs of remorse for not recognizing or caring enough to understand Jack's struggles, especially when Jack had been supportive of him during his time of immense grief. Could Jack ever forgive him?

# Chapter 2

A sentence from a popular romantic novel states, 'It is a truth universally acknowledged, that a single man in possession of a good fortune must be in the need of a wife.'

Whether the quote was accurate or not, many people believed that Grant required a partner – preferably a wife. Women who created their perfect husband bucket lists considered Grant's association with various charities an advantage. Besides being a member of the Priestly family, who were all noted for being excellent eye candy, it was also generally acknowledged that the family had an extra dollar or two. A glance into Grant's garage illustrated that point. Besides his favorite car, the Aston Martin, Grant inherited his father's midnight black Mercedes Maybach Exelero and recently purchased a metallic meteor gray Ferrari F60 Convertible. His house on Oakfield Street wasn't the largest, nor was it the smallest. Within Rochester's population, Oakfield Street was more commonly referred to as 'millionaire row.'

Some of his male friends considered his charitable involvements a great scheme to score with women while keeping his company's name in the local news. Others had hinted, with a snide comment or two, that since he had not been in a relationship for a long while, maybe he just didn't swing that way – wink, wink.

Pulling into the Regency's underground parking, Grant checked his watch. He was fifteen minutes early. 'Not bad,' he said to himself as he locked his car.

'What's not bad?' humorously inquired a voice from the car beside him.

Turning around, Grant saw Kenneth Ward, a fellow HMA committee member, approaching him. Switching his briefcase to the other hand, Grant shook Kenneth's hand. 'Since when did you take up eavesdropping, Ken?'

'Since when did you start talking to yourself?' Acknowledging the female companion by his side, Kenneth began the introductions, 'Grant, this is Daniela Weiss. She is temporarily working with the HR department until we can find someone to replace Janice. Daniela is also a part-time student at St. James going for her MBA.' Unnecessarily, he added, 'This is Daniela's first meeting.' Turning to the woman beside him, Kenneth reversed the introduction, 'Daniela, this is Grant Priestly.'

As Grant and Daniela uttered their civilities, they took a quick assessment of each other. Initially, Grant thought that when Daniela was described as a college student, she would be in her early twenties. However, he noticed his error, as he realized that Daniela was an adult student in her late thirties or maybe early forties. Daniela expected to rich and influential Mr. Priestly to greet and forget her existence. She was surprised when Mr. Priestly began to ask her questions regarding her courses. Of course, she knew who he was. His family's names and faces were regularly sprinkled on regional television and local newspapers in connection with a variety of events. She never envisaged the distinguished Grant Priestly would care about in her courses. He seemed genuinely interested. Until she realized his attentiveness to her academic activities was a result of his aversion toward her boss. Grant minimized any conversation with him. He detested Ken with his constant braggart arrogance about his fast-paced fictional life.

It was not long into the HMA meeting, that Daniela felt totally out of her depth. The meeting was a whirlwind of names, roles, and topics. She noted that quite a few companies around the area were represented.

Yesterday, when Ken told her about her new assignment, he said, 'I don't have time for HMA, but it wouldn't look good for Rowe if I dropped out. Since our company's bleeding-heart, Janice, left us I got the guys upstairs to agree that I need an assistant to take over the HMA meetings. Especially since homelessness is the trendy charity this year, it won't take much time. Just one meeting a month. That's all I do. I'll introduce you around tomorrow,' he added graciously.

About twenty persons were seated around the conference table. Even with the agenda in front of her, the participants seemed to begin on one subject and then switch to another topic. Daniela gave up trying the follow the conversion. She was shocked back into reality when she heard Ken volunteering her to be a member of the Autumn Campaign. Daniela stared in astonishment at her boss. As if he could feel her eyes boring a hole into him, he turned to her and whispered confidentially, 'Don't worry about being on the committee; I know you'll do a good job.'

'I don't even know what the Autumn Campaign does!' Daniela hissed to her boss in exasperation.

Smiling at her, Ken said casually, 'I'm not quite sure either, but you are a very ingenious person. Or so I have been told. If Priestly is involved, it would look good for Rowe to be involved too.'

Realizing that she had no idea what she was in for, Daniela answered Ken' backhanded compliment with a shaky, 'Thanks.'

# Chapter 3

Daniela was glad the HMA meeting was scheduled at the end of the day so that she was able to stop at Tops Supermarket on her way home. Arriving at her rental townhouse, Daniela attempted to carry everything in one trip. She swung her purse over one shoulder, and her bookbag tote stuffed with textbooks went over the other shoulder. Looking at the three bags of groceries, she decided to stuff them into two bags that would leave her with a free hand to open the front door. Grabbing the bags by their plastic handles, she was pleased that juggling wasn't a problem until she reached the door. Attempting to insert the key into the lock, Daniela felt a bag starting to slip. She quickly thought, 'What would get hurt the least if it fell? The purse and tote dropped in the snow as she unlocked the door.

'Has it started to snow again?' called out a male voice.

Recognizing the voice of her ex-husband, Daniela angrily ignored the question as she put the groceries on the hall table and lifted the tote and purse out of the snow. As she closed the door, she demanded. 'What are you doing here?'

In an injured tone, Steve said, 'I thought you might like to have the fireplace started. The temperature has dropped since yesterday.'

'Steve, I can start my own fire in my own fireplace. How many times have I told you to call before you come over?'

Picking up one of the grocery bags from the hallway, he set it on the kitchen counter and began to put away the contents. 'Until I believe that you don't want to see me anymore.'

'Steve, read my lips. We are divorced – finalized – legally. We are not married!'

Unfazed by Daniela's apparent hostility, Steve opened the refrigerator and put the milk on the shelf. 'That is by your choice, Sweetheart, not mine. I still believe you love me.'

Realizing the unproductiveness of any further discussion, Daniela gave up. 'Look, Steve, I have had a busy day. I'm going to pour myself a glass of wine, take my book, and soak in a nice, quiet bathtub. When you get bored, let yourself out.'

'Do you want me to scrub your back?'

'No!' Putting her plans into action, she locked the bathroom door. Daniela felt the soothing, warm water run over her fingers while she poured in her favorite bath oil. Lying back in the tub, she heard the doorknob being turned. 'The door is lock, Steve, go away.'

Coaxing, Steve said, 'You used to like me to scrub your back. Or are there any other parts of your body you would like me to rub? Remember how good it felt?'

'I never liked you scrubbing my back,' she lied. Finally, Daniela heard his footsteps fade as they moved away from the door. What a mistake it was for her to give him a house key for emergencies. When Daniela and Steve announced that they were divorcing and the house was on the market, it shocked both families and friends, especially since there seemed to be no anger or hostility during the breakup. For the first six months of the divorce, the number one question between mutual friends and family members was, 'Do you know why they split up?' Neither Daniela nor Steve would give any reason for the dissolution of the marriage.

Defiantly, Daniela opened her book, and took a sip of wine, forcing herself to relax. Unfortunately, this was one of the few times a good romance novel failed to hold her interest. Her mind kept drifting to Steve and the resentment of him being in her house. Steve was always charming and, in his way, considerate of her. His major flaw was that he could not understand why she would be upset if he drifted out of his marriage vows occasionally. He had been open about his 'oops' with a sense of humor. When Daniela found out about his affairs, he thought since his lapses occurred away from where they lived and were unknown by everyone but Daniela, it was an acceptable arrangement. To Daniela, it was not acceptable.

Daniela and Steve had met while attending RIT. Daniela was in her first year and majoring in business management. Steve was also enrolled in business but was specializing in the financial field. He always had a killer smile and a charismatic personality. He could be serious when he required. He rarely thought it was required.

Daniela dated her charming boyfriend for a year when he suggested going to Las Vegas for a long weekend. Neither of them was flushed with cash, but a holiday sounded perfect after their exams. Daniela's placatory personality dove-tailed nicely with Steve's Peter Pan attitude. While in Las Vegas, Steve proposed. With rare planning, he brought an engagement ring with matching wedding bands. He proposed by saying that women were not the only ones who could multi-task. Engagement and wedding within twenty-four hours, how much more efficient could a couple be? With optimism about what their future could be like for them, she agreed. They returned to Rochester as Mr. and Mrs. Stephen Collins.

After an incredible wedding reception party, they settled into married life. It was decided since Steve had only one more year left for his master's degree and Daniela had three more years. She would postpone the completion of her education until they were financially established.

Their plans were working with only small hiccups. There were instances when Daniela felt like Steve's mother. The number of times he spent doing house chores was almost non-existent. Daniela didn't mind as long as he was working toward their future goals. Unlike some of their friends, Steve never prevented her from visiting her family or friends. He encouraged it. How could she tell him no when he would go out for an occasional evening with his friends or visit his family? His family lived in Ohio. She had only met them once at their wedding reception. It seemed that the times when he decided to visit his family in Ohio were the times she had made plans that couldn't be broken.

Just before their first anniversary, while checking his jeans pockets before putting them in the laundry, she found a crumpled piece of paper. Smoothing it out, the feminine handwriting said – Love You Always. Daniela felt her world shattered. She was angry, hurt, and too embarrassed to tell anyone about the note. A few days later, at dinner, Daniela laid the wrinkled piece of paper on Steve's plate.

Steve picked up the note at looked at his wife's face. 'I wondered where that note went.' There were a few minutes of silence. Daniela couldn't believe her ears. Steve was nonchalant over the piece of paper. 'I'm starving and dinner smells ….'

Daniela interrupted, 'Is that all you have to say!' She demanded. Tears began to well up in her eyes. Steve got up, walked around the table, pulled her up from her chair, and put his arms around the sobbing figure.

'Dani, what is wrong? That silly note.' She couldn't believe her ears. 'Darling, the last time I was home, my cousin, Linda, remember you met her at our reception. She was totally upset because her husband just come out of the closet. And he was going to move in with his boyfriend. Linda and I have always been friends.' Pushing up her face with his fingertip, he kissed her gently. 'Sweetie, it wasn't what it looks like.'

Daniela's thoughts were swirling in her mind. Was he lying? Was he not?

'Dani, you are the best wife any man could ever have. I am so sorry that I hurt you. Linda didn't want me to say anything until she told the rest of the family. I guess I could understand her reasoning. But I should have told you. I am sorry.'

For the next minute, Daniela leaned against her husband, attempting to collect her thoughts. Steve handed her a napkin to wipe her eyes, 'You may need this. To make up for being a thoughtless jackass, I'll do the dishes tonight while you take a bath. Dani, I am really sorry that I hurt you.

Reluctantly, Daniela accepted his story. The next time Steve and Daniela visited his family, she inquired about Linda. Steve's mother said that Linda and Michael were divorced, and Linda moved out of state. Steve gave his wife a knowing wink.

For the next five years, the Collins had a traditional relationship. Steve completed his master's and started working at a job with a decent paycheck. They bought their first house, which fit in with their lifestyle. Daniela had suspicions about some of Steve's activities. However, when they were together, they were in sync and enjoyed themselves. Both agreed to not have any children for a couple more years.

It was a lovely autumn day when Daniela's car needed to go to the garage for its winterizing. She dropped off Steve at work so that she could use his car for the day. Steve was working late. If his housekeeping chores were minimal, keeping his car tidy was non-existent. Daniela decided to get his car washed and valet. When the shiny, clean car was pulled around, the car washer handed her a charge card. With his heavy accent, he explained, 'Ma'am, we found the card under the seat. It must have fallen.'

Daniela felt the gut punch again. She took the card. The card contained only her husband's name. The start date on the card began three years previously. She thanked the man and gave him his tip.

Steve greeted his wife with the usual kiss and was pleased with his cleaned vehicle. Daniela had a role to play until after dinner. Steve excused himself because he had work to do in his home office. After about thirty minutes, Daniela walked in with the card in hand and laid it on the desk beside her husband.

The look on Steve's face was one of the rare times that he looked confused. 'Your card fell between the car seats,' Daniela said calmly.

Trying to brave it out, Steve responded, 'Thank god you found it. I couldn't remember where I had left it.

'Why do you have it?'

'Because there are times when I want to buy something special for you, but I'd rather not have it show up on our joint account.'

'Excellent. Let's pull up the account - online.'

'I don't have the account online.'

'Stephen, don't lie to me. Bank statements are not delivered here. It isn't from the bank where we have our joint account. And don't tell me that you have the statements mailed to you at work. And don't say you forgot your password or tomorrow, both of us are going to the bank to have them print out the statements.'

Steve could see the anger on his wife's face. He was confounded. Rarely has he seen her this way and never at him. He was sure he could calm her down. Reluctantly, he pulled his account and clicked on the transaction pages. It took Daniela a very few seconds to realize most of the transactions were for motel rooms and restaurants in Ohio and Pennsylvania. The silence was heavy as Steve waited for the explosion he knew was coming.

There was no explosion. Daniela went into their bedroom. Steve decided that it would be safer if he slept in the spare bedroom. Overnight, Daniela realized that Steve would never change. She explained at breakfast that they would be getting a divorce. Daniela told him that nothing would be said about his extra-marital hobby. Humbled and looking like a sad puppy, Steve agreed to the divorce. But he promised he would win her back. He even helped Daniela fix up her townhouse when she moved out of the marital house. Their house went up for sale. Steve remained living in it until it was sold. Steve repeatedly postponed signing the divorce papers for nearly three years until Daniela's attorney finally discussed it with Steve's attorney.

'Why didn't I get back my house key?' she thought as she interrupted reading her book in the middle of a romantic ride fading into the moonlight by the hero and his lady.

She was just too exhausted to deal with getting the key back tonight.

After their divorce was final a little more than a year, Daniela's first goal was to complete her interrupted education. Working full-time and going to school part-time was a difficult adjustment to make without having Steve complicating her life any further. Darn, why couldn't she forget all his nice qualities and remember just his rotten habits?

Thinking of Steve brought her back to the reason she was stressed. Damn Ken for volunteering her for this new project. Daniela mostly enjoyed her job as a junior marketing analyst. Initially, she thought the job would be a secretarial position with a glorified title. As time went by, she found out that she liked the work. Daniela had been in the position for just over two years. She liked her co-workers even though Ken's attitude toward female employees was a male throwback to the Dark Ages. The major disadvantage of working at Rowe Agency was that there was limited opportunity for job advancement. Most of the staff had been in their positions for years. She thought ominously that one of them would have to literally die before she could be promoted. When she reached that conclusion, Daniela decided this would be the best time to complete her business degree programs. For the last year, she was taking two classes per semester. Even though most of the other students in her classes were fifteen years younger, she was comfortable interacting with them.

Daniela compelled her eyes to continue reading the novel. 'As he wrapped his arms around her, Piers whispered, 'I promise I will always take care of you until the end of time...'

Dreams in a fictional world were not helping her today. The book hit the bathroom door as Daniela tossed it out of the tub. 'I would like to find someone who wants to take care of me,' she thought as she stood up in the tub to finish with a warm shower. 'Preferably with no strings attached.'

A knock on the door interrupted her thoughts, 'Are you alright?' Steve asked. 'What fell?'

With a resigning sigh, Daniela continued applying hair conditioner to her shoulder-length brown hair. She answered, 'I'm fine. I just dropped my book.'

'Honestly, Dani, you are the only person I know who can read and take a shower at the same time. When you get out, I'll have supper for you.'

Daniela tried to swallow the frustration rising inside of her. Steve is trying so hard to be nice to her. Daniela did not want Steve to be nice; she wanted him to go away. Give her some breathing room. He was easier to deal with when they were fighting, but how could she be cruel to someone who, in his own way, still loved her?

Putting her damp hair into a scrunchy band, she pulled on worn-out blue sweatpants and an over-washed sweatshirt. Stuffing her feet into a comfortable pair of slippers, Daniela leery walked down the narrow hallway into the living room. Steve had pulled her coffee table in front of the fireplace. He elegantly set the table with the dinner service she received from her grandmother. 'What is this?' Daniela tried to act cross but was secretly impressed by his effort.

Coming from the kitchen, Steve carried two plates. 'You sounded tired, so I whipped up some pasta. Do you want to grab the glasses? They are on the counter.'

'Steve, thanks for making supper, but I don't have time to clean up after dinner. I really have a lot of work to do tonight. You have to leave right after we eat.'

'Sweetie, I will clean up while you study. I don't mean to make a pest of myself but I was just thinking about you today, and I knew you didn't have classes tonight so.....,' his explanation trailed off as he served up the pasta.

The warmth of the flames and the fragrant bath oils, in addition to the luxurious feeling of not cooking, began to take its toll on Daniela. She didn't want to argue. She decided to compromise and would go to work early tomorrow morning to do her remaining homework before class. That would be her traded off for a few hours of blissful peace.

# Chapter 4

When the alarm went off the next morning, Daniela angrily pushed Steve's arm away. Once again, he had got his way, and the worst part was that she had let him. 'Get up, Steve, I'm going to be late for work.'

Drowsily, Steve tried to put his arm around her again and pulled her back beside him. 'It would be easier if you would let me have maybe two hangers and one dresser drawer.'

His words acted like a splash of cold water. 'No way, Pal, it took me too long to get you out to let you back in again.'

Steve sat up on the side of the bed, rubbing the sleep from his eyes, 'But, Dani, you have to admit we never argued in bed.'

The pleasing warmth of the previous evening was gone. 'Yes, we did argue, but you never heard me. I'm going to take a shower.'

Over the running water, Daniela heard the bathroom door open. 'Goodbye, Dani, I'm leaving for work now. I'll give you a call later.'

'Don't bother, Steve. I have meetings all day and school tonight.'

'Well, I'll talk to you whenever. Love 'ya, Sweetheart.'

'I'm not sweet!' Daniela yelled at the empty doorway.

Pulling into her company's parking lot two minutes late, Daniela was glad to see that she wasn't the only straggler. 'I just hate winter,' an acquaintance from the accounting department remarked conversationally to Daniela.

'Me too. Spring can't come soon enough.' Daniela replied with a grimace as she headed up the stairs to her desk in marketing. She dropped her tote filled with books and her purse on the desk. Daniela complained good-naturedly to her friend, Alicia. 'Did you ever have one of those days that you knew you would be run twenty minutes late all day?'

'What's happening this morning?'

'This morning! Ha! It started last night when I got home, and Steve was there.'

'And? Did you kick him out?' asked Alicia, remembering the pain Daniela had suffered during the previous year.

Unable to look her friend in the face, Daniela pushed her tote under the desk and opened the desk drawer to drop her purse in it. She answered, 'No.' Trying to find the words to explain why she didn't, Daniela settled for, 'Let's go out to lunch today – cheap.'

Shaking her head, Alicia could not understand why Daniela was so reluctant to put Steve permanently out of her life. 'Sure, I'll buy. You look like you could use a perk.' The ringing of Daniela's telephone interrupted any further conversation, mouthing, 'We'll talk later.' Alicia began her own day's work.

'Good morning. Rowe Agency, this is Daniela Weiss speaking. May I help you?'

'Ms. Weiss, my name is Laura Edmunds.

Mentally, Daniela began rummaging through her various acquaintances for the name 'Laura Edmunds.' The name did not ring a bell. Daniela hoped further conversation would enlighten her, and she responded tentatively, 'Good morning, Laura, how may I help you?'

'I work for Grant Priestly. He is on the HMA Committee with you. Mr. Priestly is the Chairperson of the Autumn Campaign. He thought since you are new to the HMA, it may be helpful if you had some background information and minutes from the last few committee meetings. After you have read the material and have any questions, feel free to give me a call. I have been involved with the Campaign for the last few years.'

What Grant told Laura this morning, 'Ken brought a new girl to the meeting yesterday in the place of Janice. I can guarantee she had no idea what was going on. I don't have time to get her up to speed, and god knows Ken has no idea what is going on. Could you please locate this girl?' Referring to his notebook, he said,' Her name is Daniela Weiss. She could be working for Ken, but I don't know that for sure. When you find her, can you send her some info about the Autumn Campaign? Help her out a bit. I wish Rowe would send someone else besides Ken. He is such an ass.' Before she asked, he responded to her question. 'I understand Janice has left Rowe. I wish I knew she was interested in making a move. We could have located a place for her here.'

'Do you have any initial thoughts on how Miss Weiss will fit in with the committee?'

'At this moment, better than Ken and not as conscientious as Janice. Thanks, Laura. I appreciate you helping Miss Weiss.'

Mumbling almost inaudibly, Daniela responded to Laura, 'Yes, thank you, the information would be helpful.'

Laura continued with the phone conversation, 'Would you like me to mail the stuff to you at the office or your home?' She added warmly, 'I think some of the promotional materials look better printed out than just emailing everything.'

Daniela answered gratefully, 'I appreciate any help I can receive. Could you please send them to the office? Thank you.' Before the receiver was placed back in its cradle, Ken was at her desk with a fistful of papers, and her day was off and running.

Several days passed before Daniela received an envelope with the promised information regarding the HMA. Looking over the glossy brochures and several press releases about the organization, Daniela started to read the notes from the previous meetings. During her lunch hour, Daniela googled the internet about the Autumn campaign. Taking advantage of Ken (never Kenneth) not being on his telephone, and his office empty, Daniela brought in the HMA brochures to Ken. Waving the brochures in front of him, Daniela exclaimed, 'Ken, this looks like a lot of work.'

'It is – which is why you are doing it this year since Janice left - and not me.'

'But, why? Couldn't the HR department do a better job than marketing for corporate charitable activities?'

'Sure. That is why Janice always managed it. When I started being on this Autumn thing when it was just a golf tournament to raise money, that was no problem. Then, a couple of years ago, Priestly decided it would be more appropriate to work in one of those food-giving kitchens. Dani, can you imagine me serving food to a bunch of bums? Anyways, George says the HR department is too busy this fall with some type of medical sign-ups and to delegate it. So, that's why you are on loan to HR. You're it.'

'Ken, I don't have the time.'

'Daniela, you can do it. You're the only one in the department who doesn't have outside commitments.'

'I don't have what!'

Daniela's reaction was not what Ken counted on. 'Well, everyone else is ... you know ... attached. It's not like you're married or have kids or anything.'

'Ken, I'm going to college. You know that. You signed the tuition reimbursement paperwork, and I work 40 hours a week here, and I have a social life – occasionally.'

Ken went into his autocrat technique that he developed when he knew he was in the wrong. He looked away from her as he picked up his pen and began to write, 'I see that I have misunderstood your goals within this company, Daniela.' Daniela glared at him as he continued his tête-à-tête in which she knew she had no part. 'I considered that this program would be a good opportunity to get more involved with other businesses in the community besides assisting you in your future corporate goals.' Pausing for a few seconds, he added, 'Of course, if this is too much for you, I am sure HR could spring for a work-study student to assist you for – let's say for the next four months.

Three days later, recounting the conversation with her girlfriend over their rare Saturday morning get-together, Daniela finished, 'When I said I appreciated the opportunity and asked him if the HMA decides to have another golf tournament, can he manage the event instead of me. Ken said, 'Of course. Anything to help you out. What a line of bull that guy has! So now, in addition to everything else I have going on, there is this stupid HMA.' Sighing, she added, 'Actually, the work that the HMA does sounds good but….'

Their conversation was interrupted with, 'Mommy! Mommy! Mommy! Sarah won't let me watch the Superfriends,' screamed six-year-old Allan, running into the kitchen. Sighing, Cindy rose from the kitchen table, 'Pour yourself another cup of coffee while I settle those two down.'

When Cindy returned, she changed the conversation to more personal matters, 'Have you heard from Steve lately?'

'Only once since the night he slept over. He brought me a Christmas present. Or a non-Christmas present, as he called it. Honestly, Cindy, I don't know why I let him.'

Laughing at her friend's rarely serious face. 'You can't say that Steve got you a Christmas present and not tell me what it is!'

Looking guilty, she responded, 'It was a day at the spa gift certificate.'

Laughing even louder she asked, 'Was it for two?'

'Yes, but I haven't redeemed it,' she said defensively.

Cindy filled her friend's coffee mug again. 'Back to your original question. That is an easy answer, he has always been able to get his way with you. He acts like a lost, sad little boy. You have this mothering instinct a mile wide, and you have to make him feel better. What you need to do is to tell him 'No' and stick to it,' she advised.

'But I remember the good times.' Absentmindedly, after pouring in the milk, Daniela began stirring her coffee, watching the spoon make light brown swirls. 'Unfortunately, I don't think there was a week that went by that we didn't have at least one fight.' With a non-humorous laugh, she added, 'I wish ....'

The arguing of the children interrupted the conversation again and brought Daniela back to reality as Cindy once again jumped up from the table and said, 'I hate January. The weather is too crummy for the kids to go out and run off their energy and spring seems too far away.' Looking at her despondent friend, Cindy remarked, 'Dani, you did the right thing divorcing Steve. He isn't good for you. He manipulates you terribly. The more you tried to stand on your own, the more he tried to dominate you by acting like the child that he is.'

As Cindy returned to the living room again, Daniela remarked under her breath, 'He is a good person.' Looking at the clock, Daniela rose to leave.

Seeing her friend gathering her purse and jacket, Cindy begged her to stay. 'At 11:00, Jeff is coming to pick up the kids this afternoon for his visitation. And Tony is still in New Orleans for his business. Stay. For once, the house will be quiet.'

'No, I'm sorry but I can't. Terry is having her birthday party today and I have to get some errands done. I would also like to get some homework done before I go over to Jane's house. Can you believe it that Terry is now five years old?'

Knowing each other for over ten years, Cindy and Daniela were acquainted with each other's family. No longer protesting, Cindy shook her head, 'How time flies. I can still remember Jane's baby shower. Does your mother still hover over her?'

'Constantly. I don't know how Jane puts up with it. Mom drives me nuts after a few hours with her constant criticism. Mom has raised her kids. She should let Jane handle Terry. Jane isn't going to make any more or any less mistakes than any other parent.' Shaking her head, Daniela began to zip up her jacket.

Watching her, Cindy asked quietly, 'Can I assume that your mother still doesn't accept your divorce?'

'What an understatement! Steve could do no wrong in her eyes, and I can do no right.' Concluding the topic, Daniela added, 'Oh, well. That's life. Cindy, next Wednesday, when Jeff has the kids, let's go out to supper. Will Steve...I mean...Tony let you?'

'No problem, we'll talk later.' Opening the door, Daniela looked at the snow silently burying her car in the driveway. Daniela said, 'You know, Cindy, I do hate the cold and snow.'

Hugging her naturally buoyant friend, Cindy said encouragingly, 'Dani, cheer up. Things always have a habit of working out. And you will find someone who deserves you. Did you think three years ago that I would meet Tony, fall in love, and we would get married?'

'And who was the happiest person at your wedding? Besides, I don't want to get married.' Daniela said firmly. She was sincerely pleased that her friend was content with her life, but Dani wouldn't have married Tony if he was the last male on earth.

Cursing the snow and ice-covered roads, which made driving so exhilarate and terrifying, Daniela turned to her favorite oldie radio station. Her mind drifted to Cindy and their conversation. Daniela began to reflect on the men in her life. She had her fair share. Except for Steve, they had been male pals. She still had two male friends whom she saw sporadically socially and who had been in her life for years. Friends with benefits. It is nice to be middle age. Whomever she decided to be intimate with was no one's business but hers.

For as long as Daniela had known Greg, his marriage had been on and off several times. When Greg and his wife separated, Dani and Greg began to have casual dates. When the Bruens resumed their marriage, Greg and Daniela remained friends. They would meet occasionally or several months would pass before they would connect in person. The relationship was usually checking in with each other by phone, text, or emoji. Often, Daniela felt that she was a sounding board for Greg. She listened to his frustrations and anger regarding his job, his wife, or one of his four children. Daniela tried not to interfere in his marriage; nevertheless, she felt, in a small way, she helped the relationship. When Greg related various incidents, Daniela would add a suggestion or two from another point of view. Because she was not the enemy, sometimes he listened. Why did she remain friends with Greg? The first reason was because she did enjoy sharing a bed with him. Secondly, they shared a massive interest in science and sci-fi. Very few of her friends had an interest in Star Wars, Star Trek, the hypothesis of travel through space, or living on other planets. When he was in an optimistic frame of mind, conversations sparkled between them. Most of the time, she understood why his wife had left him.

Her other gentleman friend was Paul. He was truly happily divorced with no plans for a permanent relationship, which suited Daniela perfectly. It is great being in your forties, she thought. I can sleep with whom I want and not pretend that it is anything more than for pleasure. Defiantly, she added, it is no one's business but my own. Greg and Paul understand that I don't want the responsibilities of love or marriage, only friendship, and I don't have to promise them anything in return.

'But someday it would be nice to be in love again, to fall in love. What a silly concept,' she complained to the radio. The radio answered with another song about heartfelt love, and Daniela lapsed into a daydream. The lapse only remained until she pulled into the shopping center parking lot.

A mental image of running into the perfect mate while in the freezer aisle or the dry cleaners, which was her next stop, caused Daniela to suppress a case of the giggles. Checking her hair in the rearview mirror, Daniela scolded her reflection, 'You have been watching too many commercials. To quote one of her teenage nieces, 'I need to get a life.'

# Chapter 5

'Alicia?' Daniela inquired, leaning over Alicia's desk. Alicia turned her head to show her friend she was on the telephone. Daniela tried to not look as impatient as she felt.

'Alright, Mr. Sherring, I will have Mr. Zimmerman give you a call as soon as he returns to the office.' Replacing the telephone receiver, Alicia asked her friend, 'What gives? I thought you would be gone by now.'

'I should be. That stupid HMA meeting starts in half an hour, and I still have to drive down to the Regency. Could you do me a big favor? Ken needs the confirmation to the Close Brothers sent out by the end of today. Could you please, please, please, do it for me?' Daniela plead. 'And pick up his calls this afternoon? I wish he would hire that part-timer for me like he promised!!!'

Alice responded with a grimace to Ken's commitments. 'Sure, no problem. You better get going.'

'Thanks, Alicia, I owe you one.' She said over her shoulder as she raced out the door.

Daniela's heart skipped a beat as she tentatively pushed open the door into the conference room. The attendees were already seated as Mr. Priestly tapped the side of his water glass for silence. Daniela attempted to slide unobserved into the room, looking for an empty seat. Feeling extremely self-conscious and mentally cursing Ken for putting her on this committee, Daniela could not locate an available chair.

'Ms. Weiss, there is a chair over there.' Mr. Priestly said, breaking the silence.

Feeling the blood rush to her face, Daniela remarked acquiescently, as she felt what seemed to be a thousand eyes staring as she made her way to the chair, 'I guess making a quiet entrance is not my forte.' A few chuckles broke the awkwardness, and the meeting began.

By listening and watching, Daniela was learning more about the HMA committee members. Several more identities became clearer. Today, she counted sixteen other people at the table. Grant Priestly was the Chairperson, Karen Henderson was the secretary, Ryan somebody or other was the Treasurer and Daniela had no idea who was the Vice-President. Father Woodard was the Area Director of the three homeless shelters. Daniela was surprised at the variety of community activities that resided under the HMA umbrella.

A substantial number of local businesses were represented. Her employer, Rowe, Matterson, and Laison Agency were small potatoes compared to some of the other companies. There were attendees from two manufacturing plants, the regional telephone company, the electric & gas company, one of the five local hospitals, two churches, a bank, and a couple of law firms besides Priestly's. She listened intently to the various current reports. Before she realized it, the two-hour meeting was concluding.

'Would it be any problem for the members of the Autumn Campaign to meet here on the 18th? It is on a Tuesday at 3:00 pm. We can begin to start working on the details discussed in the proposal.' Mr. Priestly explained as he looked at the attendees. Various members nodded their assent and began marking down the date in either their electronic calendars or notebooks. Daniela paused, with pen in hand, looking around the table when she heard. 'Ms. Weiss, will you be able to make the meeting?'

Once again, Daniela felt the blood rushing to her cheeks. This time, she couldn't think of any witty comebacks and replied, 'Yes. No problem with the date.' Was Mr. Priestly deliberately attempting to humiliate her?

'Good. Can someone motion the meeting to be adjourned?' A voice responded. 'Seconded.' Another voice agreed. 'This meeting is hereby adjourned. We will see some of you on the 18th and the rest at the next meeting.' Individual conversations began as the members gathered their belongings to leave the room.

Daniela felt conspicuous by not talking to any other members as she tried to leave this uncomfortable place. She gathered her notebook and shoved it in her tote bag. 'I'm sorry if I embarrassed you, Ms. Weiss,' said the familiar voice.

Turning around and facing Mr. Priestly, Daniela felt a wave of anger. Trying to keep the tone humorous, Daniela replied, 'Then what were you trying to do, Mr. Priestly?'

'Help you find a chair and find out if the 18th meeting would be convenient for you. You looked like you may have had a conflict with the date and this being the first meeting, I thought it would be advantageous if you would be able to attend.'

Daniela felt the rush of anger recede as quickly as it rose. Picking up her pen, she dropped it in her purse. 'I apologize if I misunderstood your motives. I was trying so hard to blend into the woodwork, and you... and, well, it didn't work out that way.' Out of curiosity, she asked, 'What would you have done if I couldn't attend on the 18th?'

A quick laughter of understanding was followed by, 'I had several dates that it could have been moved to. Ken recommended that you could manage any event to perfection.' He saw her grimace at the mention of Ken's name. 'But I doubt if we will see Ken at the dinner this year.' Ruefully, Daniela agreed. As Grant walked to the doors, he turned to face her, 'I hope I didn't scare you away.'

'I'll be there, Mr. Priestly.'

'Good. And since we will be working together, only a few of my older employees call me Mr. Priestly.' Pushing open the door, he added, 'I realize that at first few meetings, everyone's name must seem like a blur, my name is Grant.'

Daniela could feel her face becoming flushed again. She was angry with herself since she generally had a response to any situation. All she could say was, 'My name is Daniela,' and felt even more foolish. Of course, he already knew her name.

'I look forward to working with you, Daniela.' With a quick farewell smile, Grant hailed another committee member. Jeff what-is-his-last-name, and Grant were deep into a conversation as they walked down the hallway.

When she unlocked her car and turned the key to start the engine, within her mind, she began her silent conversation with herself. Mr. Priestly, no...Grant did not seem to be the rich snob she first imagined. He seemed to be a nice man and easy on the eyes. She had known very little about him, so she googled … hmmm, maybe several times, but that really wouldn't be considered stalking, would it? She chuckled as she continued her internal conversation. Not stalking, more like research. Besides indulging in a little fantasy about the handsome, rich, and impossible-to-have Grant Priestly wasn't hurting anyone. Attempting to divert her mind, Daniela defiantly turned on the radio. The words were drifting out to her. 'I want to get to know you...Yes, I do...' Laughing at the timing, Daniela caught sight of her reflection in the rear-view mirror. The laughter stopped.

Daniela realistically looked at herself. She had to admit to herself even though she did not feel her age at forty-one she was starting to get into that mature stage. Thinking of all the twenty and thirty-year-old folks who constantly worked out and had perfect bodies and perfect young families, Daniela felt old. She laughably admitted to her friends that she was exercise deficient. Her light brown, highlighted shoulder-length hair seemed to always have a 'bad hair' day. At this moment, there was no gray; but she hated the mousy brown and enjoyed the luxury of going to a salon and being pampered several times a year. Her figure was full, about twenty pounds fuller than she would have liked. She had been told several times that her deep brown eyes were considered one of her best features as they peered at the world through wire-framed spectacles.

Being married at twenty-five and divorced at thirty-five, she felt like she was always going through some type of marital or budgetary crisis.

It didn't seem fair that most men she knew seemed to be aging gracefully and were more financially comfortable, while she only felt older and poorer.

'Good Gosh!' Daniela exclaimed out loud as she pulled into her driveway. 'Enough of this self-pity.' Looking at the dark, snowy January sky with just a sliver of the moon shining, and it wasn't even six o'clock yet, Daniela wished that spring would make its appearance, and quickly too.

The romance department in Daniela's life was in a temporary lull. On one hand, she didn't mind because several other things were taking priority. Then, on the other hand, she did miss chatting with her male friends. She didn't miss them enough to contact them. To replace her real-life romantic activities, unconsciously, she had created her 'Grant Priestly' fantasies. Why were they happening? Maybe because she was encountering a rare moment of romantic wasteland and the rest of her life seemed boring. Daniela felt embarrassed over the random thoughts that would creep in at odd moments. If she seemed slightly distracted at work or with her friends, she would just remark that she had tests coming up.

On the morning of the 18th, Daniela found herself carefully picking out her clothes. The day seemed to drag on until she left for the meeting. Feeling slightly more at ease, Daniela was able to exchange a few pleasantries with other HMA members. The meeting passed smoothly thanks to Laura sending her the past meeting notes. Daniela mostly listened, absorbing HMA information, and began to understand the various members committee's roles. The meeting was adjourned before she noticed that Grant hadn't said a word to her. Nor did he even look at her. Her fantasies came to a crashing halt. Daniela left the meeting feeling hurt and a little angry.

It wasn't until she unlocked the door to her house did she note with black humor that her feelings of the blues were a result of her over-the-top romantic fantasies. To be honest, she was also embarrassed that at forty-one years old, she had such silly, nonsensical fairy tale thoughts. At previous meetings, Grant Priestly had been friendly and polite. He was doing his job by trying to make her fit into a group that needed to be unified within a short period of time.

She had built nothing into something. Feeling foolish, and fortunately, only Daniela knew how big of a fool she was, she picked up the telephone and invited Paul over for a late supper. Paul arrived with Chinese take-out and spent the night.

In the morning, Daniela knew she used Paul to take care of her battered ego, which her stupid fantasies had created. As Paul exited from the shower, Daniela was dressing for work. Paul began styling his graying hair in the dresser mirror when he caught sight of Daniela's half-dressed reflection. 'Nice breasts.'

Accepting the remark for what it was, Daniela answered, 'I'm glad you enjoyed them.' Deciding to confess, 'Paul, you know I was just using you last night.'

Undisturbed, Paul continued to dress, 'For any particular reason.'

'My ego got hurt yesterday and you always make me feel better.'

'Do you feel better?'

Smiling at the memories of the previous evening, Daniela replied, 'Yes. Definitely.'

'Then no problem. I was using you too. I was extremely horny last night.' Pulling Daniela close to him, he reached around and cupped her bottom. After a lingering kiss, Paul released her, and they continued dressing. 'How about supper tonight?'

Daniela answered regretfully, 'No, Sweetie, I have my class tonight. How about Saturday night?'

'Sounds good. Movie?'

'It's a deal.' Daniela watched Paul for a moment as he was putting on his coat and gloves. Thinking of what a good friend he was, she impulsively called, 'Paul?'

Paul looked curiously at her, 'Yes?'

'Paul, do you know you are a sweetheart?'

Walking back to her, Paul dropped a kiss on top of her head, 'Tell me again on Saturday. I'll call you later.'

# Chapter 6

'The month of March was true to its cliché; it came in like a lion and out like a lamb. Or was it the other way around?' Grant asked himself. Regardless of the saying, the gloomy, dark-spirited days of winter were receding, and the signs of spring began to embellish the landscape.

Grant was one of those rare people who enjoyed returning to his office on Mondays. He had developed a firm rule of not going to the office on Saturdays and Sundays. His home office was created to analyze future corporate plans, review the most recent business projects' performances, and examine current law cases. Of course, the human resources staff were hired to analyze corporate business performances. On the other hand, the habit of reviewing Priestly Enterprises' activities on Sunday nights was a legacy from when only his parents managed the firm. As far back as he could remember, while Grant and his siblings were watching The Wide World of Disney, his parents sat around the kitchen table and developed tasks and agendas for the upcoming week.

After his parent's divorce, father and son continued the Sunday evening's legacy. At different times, his other siblings would be included but none exhibited interest in either the law or the running of the family business. Russell had found a kindred spirit in his eldest son. Grant was barely in high school when his father began discussing all aspects of Priestly Enterprises with him on their special Sunday evenings.

Upon Russell's remarriage and starting his first year at Harvard, Grant felt a loss when the Sunday review sessions, out of necessitate, had to be curtailed. When Grant came home for long weekends and holidays, father and son looked forward to their traditional evening. Even when Russell started to transition into retirement, the evenings continued until...

As the door automatically opened into Priestly Enterprises, Grant greeted the security guard whose office was located to the left of the front doors. Brenda was not due to be behind the receptionist's desk for another 45 minutes.

Grant enjoyed corporate synergy. He encouraged managers to think outside of traditional business ethos with a diversification of innovative ideas. Three years ago, when the well-organized Laura, requested every departmental meeting's date, time, and location, the term 'pedantic' besides other less polite terms, was used for her request. Grant began to appear unexpectedly at various meetings. Initially, his presence unsettled most of the employees. Whether the meeting was with the mailroom employees or the IT project management team, there was no forewarning if he would attend.

As Russell began to take more time away from the business, he gave Grant more responsibility. He began to have grave doubts when Grant wanted to prototype his initial concept of attending meetings at every level. Grant loved his father, but he knew his father rarely listened to any opinion that countered his viewpoints. Russell started to moan over the fact that his son's management style was too soft. The senior Priestly believed that employees below a certain pay grade were a waste of his valuable time. There were parts of the office building that Russell had not ventured into since the grand opening. Russell stated repeatedly that becoming too familiar with employees was just asking for trouble.

Grant's attendance at meetings brought several benefits and only a few downsides. Initially, his unexpected appearance was uncomfortable to everyone in the room. After being introduced to the attendees, he would not offer comments or suggestions. Rarely he would make any notes. He stopped taking notes after he noticed as soon as his pen touched his notebook, dead silence filled the room. After that first disastrous meeting, he learned an important lesson. Now, after a meeting, he would thank everyone for allowing him to attend and leave. The unparalleled Laura would book a space near the meeting room so that Grant could write out his thoughts. He preferred not to verbally record his thoughts because he did not want to take the chance of being overheard. The first few months of the meetings frightened everyone until several positive actions began to appear. Short memos materialized thanking certain employees for their original ideas or their better processing methods. When appropriate, there were also memos to department leaders for developing a well-functioning team. What was even more surprising was that no negative memos were received. Conversely, during this period, several employees' positions were modified.

During one of his recent Sunday weekly reviews, he was surprised that the employee turnover rate had declined substantially from the previous year. Grant enquired from Brad Stanowski, the VP of Human Resources, what had changed. Brad stated that based on exit interviews, focus groups, and annual review reports, the strategies established the previous year for reducing expensive employee turnovers were beginning to become effective. The three-prong approach of suitable salary, including benefits, training to ensure the necessary job knowledge, and loyalty to employees, when appropriate, was working.

Russell put his own interpretation on his son's management style, and it was not always positive. Russell preferred to believe when no one was told in advance if Grant attended staff meetings, employees would come well-prepared. The fear of not being prepared would trigger fears of being terminated or demoted. Increased efficiency from his employees at no additional financial outlay was Russell's primary objective.

Taking the short trip on the elevator from the receptionist area to his office, Grant let the feeling of being overwhelmed by the stress in his life envelop him. His father's heart attack, then his unexpected Covid virus death last year, in addition to the extra business workload that had been increasing with no relief in sight, made Grant feel isolated.

Besides keeping abreast of the business activities, his family's affairs were taking their toll. His paternal grandmother had developed an intense reliance upon Grant since the death of his father. Her dependency increased substantially until she became agitated if he did not visit her at least several times a week.

Russell was Lucille Priestly's only child. Grant and his siblings held a family conference days after their father's death to discuss the best method for managing their beloved ninety-three-year-old Grandmother. Grant's two younger sisters were married and lived out of state, raising their young families. The youngest Priestly sibling, Ian, agreed to live with their Grandmother. He could be her companion and assist her when required. A day nurse was reluctantly accepted by Grandma Lucy. Determinedly she stated that she did not want a nurse to be underfoot 24/7. Ian was single and generally between homes. Whereas the rest of the family was uncertain of his capability to care for her, at this moment, there was no other choice. Despite Ian living at his Grandmother's house, Grandma Lucy still asked for Grant's company.

Besides having a place to live, Ian was being paid handsomely for providing their grandmother with companionship. Ian considered himself the creative artist genius in the family. Unfortunately, Ian had rarely sold an art piece to anyone outside the family. Internally, Ian knew that he was an underrated artistic genius. He felt sorry for people who did not understand his impressionist oil paintings.

Russell had very few positive opinions regarding his youngest son. He supposed that art had its place in the world and should be kept as a hobby, except for those who were truly talented. Ian Priestly was not one of those people. Russell did not approve of Ian's rotation of girlfriends, the substantial number of friends Ian acquired over the years, or his non-ending requests for money. Russell underwrote and promoted three one-man art shows for his son. Local art critics were wined and dined. Their positive analysis gave Ian's paintings the praises required to start him on the lowest foothold in the art world. Only a minority of people agreed with the local art critics' point of view.

Ian's lack of commitment, in as much as his lack of talent, reduced his art endeavors, in his family's opinion, to the artworks created by the Priestly's nieces and nephews.

Grant used the keypad to enter his 5th-floor corner office. The CEO's office was large enough to include, besides the usual office furniture, an adjoining personal area that contained a kitchenette and bathroom facilities. The main office possessed an additional room for the ten-person conference desk with several internet-connected monitors. Upon reaching his office, Grant placed his briefcase on the new office desk.

When Russell decided to do most of his work from home, he gifted his office to Grant. The office had been designed with ultra-sleek glass and gold furniture. When Russell worked with the architect of the Priestly Building, he wanted his CEO space to illustrate power and efficiency and encourage people not to remain in the office for too long.

The Internet monitors were added during the COVID period to accommodate governmental and human resource policies. The conference room did not seem out of place in the office suite. The office redolence with power. The kitchenette, a bathroom with a shower, and a closet containing extra clothing for those quick changes when going home were not feasible.

Grant missed his father's business savvy and companionship. Looking out of the corner office window in the state-of-the-art Priestly Enterprises office building, Grant remembered the multiple conversations with his father over the years.

Every evening before Laura left for the day, she set up the coffee maker. Grant turned on the machine and began reviewing his calendar and emails. He poured his first cup of coffee and started reading the email Adrian King from Germany.

In the 80's, Barbara and Russell Priestly hung out their Priestly Attorneys-at-Law shingle in the community where the prior Priestly family members lived. After winning three high-profile cases with significant fanfare, the law firm began to expand rapidly in a city that was also expanding rapidly. When the doors of the firm opened, it began with Barbara taking on the role of business manager. Besides their legal skills, four employees, and a few astute business contracts, Priestlys developed a solid reputation. At the same time, the business was expanding, and so was the Priestly family. The first child was Grant, followed by Eleanor, two years later Mariah, and completing the family was Ian.

Just before the death of Russell, the law firm employed 450 people inclusive of 50 plus law associates. Now, the firm's involvement included more than legal issues. Priestly Legal Firm barely entered the 1990s when Russell began creating a real estate portfolio. Before the Priestly's divorce, they decided to restructure the business.

Adrian King met Barbara Ryan as a fellow Cornell law student who shared several classes. Their friendship was cemented when they discovered both lived in West Virginia in similar small communities less than fifty miles apart. Upon graduation, Adrian's interests led him to accept a position working at a non-profit human rights organization in Washington, DC. Meanwhile, Barbara married Russell Priestly and relocated to a city in Western New York. When Adrian had a problematic case, he requested Barbara's assistance. When the Priestlys required advice from Adrian's area of expertise, he was just a speed-dialed number away. At the time, the Priestlys decided to diversify the legal business and add the very profitable commercial property management, they knew they would required additional senior management staff. Adrian King's name was on top of their recruiting dream list.

Since their student days, the Priestlys and Kings kept in touch. After Adrian married Elaine, the two families would occasionally vacation together. During a trip to Italy, Grant and Barbara offered Adrian the presidency position at Priestly Enterprises' Legal Division.

The majority of Priestly's legal department focused on corporate business affairs. Adrian's previous experiences represented individuals and organizations who could not defend themselves. Over time, he became involved in the ignominy world of human rights violations. Barbara's legal field as also in human rights until her marriage redirected her activities into the family business.

The Priestly's offer came at a time when Adrian needed to balance his excessive workload with his home life. The request came very strongly from his wife. In addition to his non-stop caseload, he was frustrated with the unnecessary Washington political drama, especially since the recent Presidential election. Politics were subtly changing when the new President considered the United States was interfering too much in other countries' politics. The major platform of the President-elect's campaign had been run concept that the 'United States is not the world's policemen.' It was not a difficult choice to accept the Priestly's offer to lead its legal division. Even after Grant and Barbara's divorce, he maintained an equilibrium with both his friend and his CEO.

Despite passing the official retirement age, Adrian continued to enjoy the challenges of his position. He had several unique corporate attributes. Not only was he one of the most qualified Human Rights attorneys in the United States, but he could evaluate new legal talent in a remarkably brief period. Rarely was he incorrect in his assessments.

While Grant was studying to pass his bar exam, Russell decided to put into action a plan he had in mind for years, incorporate all Priestly's business functions into one location. The evening before the Priestly Buildings' Grand Opening, and with no one in the facility, father and son walked through the massive, eerie emptiness of office spaces. In a rare moment of relaxed companionship, Russell laid out his plans for his son. Not just for his family's immediate future but for the Priestly dynasty. They both laughed when he said that word - Dynasty. Little did Grant realize his father truly believed that he was starting a Dynasty. Considering the members of his immediate family, Grant grimaced at the lack of material his father had to work with. Shifting his mind back to the emails at hand, Grant returned to his tasks of the day.

Laura entered Priestly Enterprises thirty minutes after her boss. She saw the closed office door and knew that he had started his day. Laura's skills had been shared between father and son. When Grant took over the corporate reins, Laura enjoyed her position even more. Grant did not have emotional outbursts like his father, which kept the employees on tenterhooks. He was kind. It seemed to be a simple word, but it was appropriate. Grant remembered most of his employee's names. When

Grant was angry, he didn't scream or use inappropriate words. Laura mused he wasn't cold-hearted; he just seemed to be - what would be a correct word? Distant? He kept everyone at a distance. As Laura turned back to her computer screen, she smiled. She thought, 'I'd much rather have him distant than yelling at me all the time like his father.'

Grant began his workday with the same routine: check his online calendar, which Laura updated for him, review any phone messages, and then surf through his emails, which required priority responses. Grant created two email accounts. His corporate account, which Laura reviewed to keep out the scams and junk emails, and his private email account. He had read the message that Adrian had sent him. Besides his empty coffee cup were notes he needed Laura to research on behalf of the case in Germany.

He had completed his first two tasks and began working on this third when Laura gave a slight tap on the door. She entered, holding a mug of coffee with the steam fogging the air above it.

He joked as he took it from her, 'What is the special occasion?' Laura's one request, or was it a demand, when she was hired was that she was not a part-time waitress fetching coffee whenever it was needed. Of course, Russell ignored the request. Grant appreciated the reason behind the request. However, there were times when Laura felt sorry for her hard-working boss and brought him a coffee.

For once, Laura seemed tongue-tied. 'Well,' she started hesitantly.

'Have a seat,' Grant invited her, suddenly realizing that this was not a common situation.

'Well,' she repeated. Then she held out her left hand. Grant noticed the engagement ring.

'Congratulations, Laura. I am assuming that it is Oliver.' Speechless, Laura nodded. 'Is this good news? Do you have a wedding date set?' Grant remarked. He was confused by her less-than-happy mannerisms.

'Yes, we set the date. Our plans are for next summer after he graduates.' She added in a rush, 'Then we are moving to England.' Silence descends in the room for a few seconds. She added softly, "I'm sorry.'

Grant smiled. 'Laura, are you sorry that you and Oliver are getting married?'

'Oh no, no, no,' she said, shaking her head. 'That I have to leave Priestly. I love working for you.'

Touched by her obvious loyalty, Grant joked, 'I don't think the commute will be too bad. Obviously, you and Oliver will be purchasing a house near Gatwick Airport.'

Laura looked up from her clasped hands and smiled, 'Obviously not,' she joked back. 'When we get to England, I will become a proper British mum. I have been watching every episode of 'Keeping Up with Appearance' and 'Dr. Who,' and scheduled to re-watch all Harry Potter movies. That should prepare me for the British culture. I hope I can pick up the accent.' Changing back to her business persona, Laura added, 'Since the wedding is planned for next year in August, I expect my last day to be sometime around May. If that is acceptable to you?'

Taking a sip of coffee, Grant nodded. 'Okay. Take time to enjoy your engagement then we can discuss how to manage the transition.'

Laura stood up and with heartfelt 'thanks,' she left the office.

'Wow,' Grant thought as he returned to his private emails. Taking a deep sip from his coffee, he saw 3 notifications that new emails had arrived within minutes of each other from Tiffany, Ian, and his half-sister, Rachel. Sighing, he thought, this is not starting off to be one of my better days.

# Chapter 7

Daniela backed out of her mother's driveway. Anger, frustration, and depression had joined her behind the steering wheel of her car as she started for home. Was she as much of a loser as her mother kept implying? Her mother didn't say it outright. The comments were always in the nature of barbed compliments. According to her mother, several of Daniela's flaws were that she was not married like her siblings that she didn't have any children like her siblings, or her secretarial job was a starter position, unlike her successful older siblings. Her mother always added, at some point in their conversation, that Daniela was not getting any younger. The pièce de résistance, her mother always ends their visit with the same comment, 'But I'm proud of you.'

She could feel the tears welling up. 'No!' She shouted to the steering wheel. Daniela started to inventory her life to prove or refute her mother's opinions. Another semester is almost completed, two more to go, work is as boring as ever, and social life is as confusing as usual. The only item new in her life was that she was developing a growing interest in the HMA which surprised her.

The Autumn Committee was created to generate revenues, as well as publicity, for the organizations' programs. Daniela spent the first couple of meetings listening to the five primary members of the committee. Her feelings of being an outsider were beginning to subside. The other HMA members were managers or directors or someone important in their business lives. The committee members were diversified both in culture and background. After recovering from her flights of fantasy, Daniela was able to view Grant Priestly objectively. He was definitely handsome and seemed to be gracious in most situations. He also had a nice sense of humor, even if it was on the dry side. The most surprising impact he made on her is that he cared about the HMA's objectives.

The Committee had three specific goals for the Autumn Event. Raising public awareness of its programs, organized an annual charity ball, and arranged for Thanksgiving meals for people who could not afford a proper meal on this day of thanks. What amazed Daniela was that, in her overcrowded life, she had volunteered to work on rotating Friday evenings at one of Father Woodward's residences for women and children. Daniela sighed as she remembered her mother's petty comments about working and not getting paid. Why was she volunteering to help those 'dirty' and 'lazy' people because it was their fault they were seeking public shelter?

Working with HMA she had learned some of the reasons why people became homeless. These reasons scared Daniela. Very few people are prepared for the negative impact of losing a job, unexpected medical issues, or a multitude of other factors that could have a financial or emotional impact on their lives. She thought about people who had real problems, a lot worse problems than an overbearing mother. Her initial thoughts of desperation began to lift. She may not have a perfect life - whatever perfect meant - but so many people had far less than she did. Making a sudden decision, Daniela turned right and headed to the Roselyn House for Women and Children. Over the last few weeks, she has been collecting toys, baby, and women's clothes from her friends' and families' overstocked closets and toy boxes. She cleaned the items and repacked them into black rubbish bags. They have been gathering in the trunk of her car. She planned on dropping them off on her next rotation day. But today, Daniela just didn't feel like going straight home;

besides, she wanted to see how Louise and little Elsa were fairing. The mother and daughter were admitted to the shelter on her rotation day last Friday night. Louise was terrified about leaving her abusive partner. Three year old Elsa clung to her mother the entire time they were being settled in.

Reaching Roselyn House, Daniela reflected on how an outdated office building could be converted into a comfortable place of refuge for twenty women and children. Opening the trunk, Daniela scooped up as many of the awkward-shaped bags as she could manage. Walking up the three steps to the front door, 'Drat!' thought Daniela as her fingers began fumbling, trying to find the door handle while juggling the bags. Just as her fingers found the doorknob, the door opened inward under its own power. The motion threw Daniela off balance. Before she could stop herself, she and the bags were sprawled on the wooden floor in the entrance hallway. 'Goddamn!' she uttered before she had a chance to look around her. She looked up and saw the startled stares of several well-dressed women and men.

Multiple voices were talking at once, 'Let me help you.' 'Oh dear, what happened?' 'Are you okay?' 'Are you hurt?'

'Oh, great,' Daniela thought to herself, 'I just love making a fool of myself in front of people.' Repeating several times, she said, 'I'm fine. I'm fine.' She kept her head down after she pushed her hair back off her face and began to gather the bags together. She heard two familiar voices.

'Daniela, are you all right?' said Claire Evans, the Director of the Shelter whom she only met once during her initial interview.

'Can I help you?' asked Grant Priestly.

For a moment, she stared at both of them. 'No, no,' she embarrassedly gathered the remaining bags together. 'I had just brought some items in. Things for the children and other stuff,' she added disjointly. The room for donations was to the right of the front door. Daniela and two others from the group carried the bags to the room. After they left the bags on the sorting table, her helpers returned to their group.

'Oh, Hanfeeh,' Daniela exclaimed to the elderly live-in social worker who resided on the premises. Hanfeeh assisted the women, temporarily housed at Roselyn, to manage the tangled mess of bureaucratic red tape necessary to help rebuild their lives. Hanfeeh resided on the premise since the building opened its doors. 'I made such a fool of myself today.'

As Hanfeeh began to open the bags, she agreed in her soft Jamaican accent. 'Well, Child, if you were going to make an entrance, that was a beaut.'

'I have more stuff in the car, but I am not going to leave this room until they are gone. Who are they?'

'Have you heard of Grant Priestly?' She continued without waiting for a response. 'He is here giving them a tour. They are from Saratoga and heard about the HMA business model and decided to check it out.' For the next fifteen minutes, Hanfeeh and Daniela worked sorting and logging in the items. Hanfeeh remarked, 'There are a lot of baby clothes and toys here.'

'Definitely,' Daniela agreed. 'For a while, most of my friends and family seemed to be popping out kids. One boy and three girls in three years.'

Looking over the top of her half-framed glasses, Hanfeeh questioned, 'None of your own?'

'Nope.'

The door opened and Grant Priestly entered with several more bags. 'Daniela, I hope you don't mind. I brought these in and closed your trunk door.' Hanfeeh moved around the table to relieve Grant of his burdens.

'I was just about to go out and get them.' Daniela said defensively.

'How did the people from Saratoga like Roselyn House?' Hanfeeh asked.

'They were interested in the entire concept.' Ruefully, he added, 'All it takes is people and money.' Changing the subject, he added, 'Daniela, I'm surprised to see you here.'

Hanfeeh looked from Grant's surprised face to Daniela's embarrassed one. Daniela never mentioned that she had met Roselyn House's primary patron. She interrupted, 'Daniela is our Friday evening carer who joined up about' looking at Daniela.

'Seven weeks ago.' Daniela responded.

'Daniela, why don't you go? Enjoy the rest of Saturday while it is dry. It is supposed to rain later on. We are almost finished sorting.' For a final dismissal, she added to Daniela, 'Tell everyone thanks for their donations. Most of it almost brand new.'

'Okay. Thanks. See you on next Friday.'

'Take Care, Hanfeeh,' said Grant as he opened the door, allowing Daniela to walk out first. Standing beside her car, Daniela was incredibly tongue-tied. She couldn't even utter the most the most inane comment. As she started to open her car door, she was aware that she looked like something the cat dragged in.

'Daniela, Do you have anything planned for the next couple of hours?'

She paused and looked at Grant, mystified. 'No. Not really. Just doing some housework.'

'I was just wondering if you had some free time. Well, I have an appointment to check out some new bedding for the shelters. If you aren't busy, maybe you would like to come with me, to keep me company? No alternative motive. I would like a woman's opinion. Besides, it is a nice day now that the rain has stopped. If you don't have anything else planned for this afternoon?' Half of Grant's brain was thinking, 'Why doesn't she say something?'

'This certainly wasn't a date. What was it? Oh, what the heck! If they found my body parts tomorrow - so be it.' Thought half of Daniela's brain. Taking the plunge, Daniela smiled and said, 'I am wearing my Saturday-running-around-looking-like-a-slob outfit.' Unbeknown to Daniela, when she smiled, her entire face lit up. Steve called it her '100 watt' smile. Every time he said it, Daniela knew it was a cliché that he had picked up somewhere. She straightened her shoulders and flashed her 100-watt smile again.

Grant responded with a smile of his own, 'I'm wearing my I'm-trying-to-impressed-clients-while-looking-casual outfit.' He opened the passenger side door for her. As Daniela sunk into the soft leather seat, she idly thought, this car probably cost as much as her house.

They traveled the forty-five minutes to a warehouse in Batavia where various styles of blankets were manufactured. Daniela couldn't remember the details of the drive, only that they laughed and chatted as if they had known each other longer than a couple of months. At the warehouse, Grant asked her opinion regarding several of the samples. They were heading back to Roselyn House so that she could pick up her car when, during a moment of silence, Grant asked. 'It's getting near dinner time. Do you want to grab a bite to eat?'

Daniela hesitated for a moment. 'I'm sorry, not tonight. I have plans.'

'No problem. It was just a shot in the dark.'

'Grant, I would like to, but I promised my brother that I would watch my nieces. Today is their anniversary.'

'Another time?'

'Of course,' Daniela was generally self-confident around the men in her life. Why did she feel like a naïve schoolgirl around Grant? Especially after the comradeship of the afternoon. Were her mother's insults residing permanently in her brain cells? After a couple of minutes of struggling with her internal thoughts, the question slipped out. 'Why?'

'Why what?' He asked, mystified.

'Why are you asking me out? Or aren't you?'

'Because I like you and want to know you better. Isn't that enough reason?'

'Not really.' For the next mile, Daniela looked miserably out the window. Why did she just act so bitchy toward Grant? He had done nothing to deserve it. Once again, her insecurities were threatening to overwhelm her emotional equilibrium. Clearing her throat, she looked at Grant's rock-hard face, staring straight ahead. The cloud of silence filled the car. 'I'm sorry,' she said softly.

'There is nothing to be sorry about. You put me in my place.'

'No,' she attempted to explain. 'I just can't understand why a person like you would want to have anything to do with a person like me.'

'What!' Grant swerved and pulled his car into a lay-by. He turned off the engine and faced Daniela. 'Okay, explain to me what you mean a 'person like me'? What am I?'

Struggling for words, Daniela couldn't say anything that would make sense to herself, much less him. The unreasonableness of her comment hit her between the eyes. 'Was I being a total ass?'

Not taking his eyes from her, Grant responded. 'Should I agree or disagree with you?'

A wry smile started. 'Feel free to agree. I deserve it. Me - who gets angry at people stereotyping other people just stereotyped you.'

'What's my stereotype?'

'Handsome, wealthy, upper-class man taking pity on…'

Impatiently, he interrupted, 'Don't forget – snob - If that is what you think.' He angrily started the car.

Daniela put her hand on his arm. 'Stop for a second.' He looked at her and turned off the engine again. 'I am truly sorry. I was having such a wonderful time with you today. I wasn't thinking about anything but here and now. But here and now just progressed to the next hours. You have your life, and I have mine. Different lifestyles except twice a month we meet. I know this sounds silly.'

'Daniela, I am not quite sure what you are trying to say. Yes, I met you through the HMA. Today, I met you at Roselyn, which was unexpected. Without a doubt, asking you to drive with me to Manns was an impulse - which, believe me - I rarely do. But I wanted to have dinner with you because you seemed to be funny and intelligent, and I enjoyed being with you.'

'I have seen you in the news.

'So?'

'With Lady Elizabeth Bodern.'

Laughter suddenly filled the car. This confused Daniela she looked at Grant. 'So you enjoy gossip.' With a quick mischievous glance in her direction, 'I didn't figure you were THAT type of a person.'

Defensively, she said, 'It was in the news, and it was implied that there was more than an evening out.'

'Liz or Lady Elizabeth Bodern is my sister's best friend. She is attempting to get her boyfriend to propose. It was a plan that she and my sister cooked up. They wanted me to do a little romancing. According to my sister, it worked. The Duke of Rufford left England yesterday and should be arriving in New York City with, if my sister is correct, an engagement ring for Liz.'

'You went along with it?'

'Sure. Why not?' He tried again, 'Does this mean that now you are not the 'other woman' you will have dinner with me?'

'I would like to, except not tonight. Besides watching the kids, I feel grubby and worst of all, I have a paper that is due on Monday. I was planning on getting it mostly finished tonight after I put the kids to bed.'

Starting the car, he pulled onto the highway. 'Daniela, I am not going to press you. I know you are busy. When we get to Roselyn, I will give you my private number. You can call me when you have a free evening. I am serious. I would like to have dinner with you. I've enjoyed your company.'

'What if you are busy when I am free?'

Mischievously, he looked at her, 'Call me and we will find out.'

# Chapter 8

Rarely did Grant act on impulse, however, he was glad that he did. He had no intention of asking Daniela to drive with him to Manns Outlet, nor did he plan to ask her out to dinner. Doing what he does best, Grant began to analyze what just happened. What set her apart from the other women he has dated? He noticed almost immediately that her face reflected her emotions. Whether she was concentrating or embarrassed, he knew. Of course, when she came crashing through the door with those black rubbish bags and landed at their feet, he had to restrain from laughing at the situation. To be honest, he felt a little guilty at that. If he had not opened the door at the same time, she would not have been thrown off balance. He was glad that it happened and enjoyed their afternoon together. Surprisingly, her knowledge of a variety of topics was similar to what interested him, from politics to the latest movies. Maybe it was because she was older than most of his female friends.

Any pleasurable feeling was erased when he saw a familiar car in front of the house. The car brandished a new dent with accompanying missing paint patches on the passenger side. He mentally sighed before entering the house. Stepping into the marble cathedral ceiling entranceway, he noticed was the opulent, exorbitant-priced chandelier was lit. The massive collection of crystals, wires, and candle-shaped light bulbs was rarely used. Grant considered the chandelier pretentious when Tiffany purchased it as a housewarming gift. He heard his brother addressing him from the conservatory, 'Bro, why don't you turn up the heat in this mausoleum?'

'I don't need to. I am not dressed like it is 90 degrees in Florida. Hello, Becca.' Both his brother and his latest girlfriend, Becca, already had drinks in their hands. When his housekeeper entered the room, Grant asked, 'Mrs Moore, may I have some ice water, please? Also, please tell Alex not to make dinner for me tonight. I forgot to tell him that I have a client's meeting at 7.'

His housekeeper's eyes did not budge from his face as she said, 'Yes, Sir.'

The last comment she heard as she closed the conservatory door was Ian complaining, 'You can't possibly have a client meeting this late on a Saturday night.'

Sylvia Moore knew full well that there was no meeting, and she did not tell Alex to cancel dinner. Ian Priestly was out of luck if he was planning on eating under this roof.

With a glass of ice water in his hand, Grant finally brought his brother's ramblings to an end by asking directly. 'Ian, I need to get ready shortly. What do you need?'

Ian faked looking hurt, 'Can't one brother visit another brother?'

'And?'

'Well, it's like this.' Grant sipped his water, waiting to see how much this was going to cost. 'The old lady has been a nag and demanding.' Grant knew his grandmother was neither. 'Becca and I need some vacation time.' Looking at Becca, he added, 'We feel we need some time off to regenerate our batteries.' Grant refrained from saying anything. Looking at his silent brother, Ian said in a rush, ' We need $10 thou to go to Thailand for a couple of weeks.'

'Ten thousand dollars!'

'Make it fifteen. I heard the prices of everything have gone up.'

'What happened to the payment which was sent into your account five weeks ago?'

'Man, I have expenses.'

'Twenty thousand dollars of expenses? You live with Gran and your alimony and child support are already paid by the estate.'

'Fine. If you want to be like that, make it an advance on the next quarter payment.'

'I can't, and I won't.'

'What the fuck are you talking about!' exploded Ian. 'You are living like a fucking king and you won't give your brother a fucking dime.'

With a strong effort, Grant remained calm. 'There was so much wrong with that statement.'

'Don't give me that my shit don't stink bullshit.' Ian interrupted. 'You don't know what it is like being stuck with that old lady day after day.'

'Didn't you just return from Hawaii two weeks ago?'

'Fuck you!' He repeated, 'Fuck you!' His glass shattered on the marble floor as he angrily threw it across the room. 'Becca, we're leaving this hellhole.' Ian stormed out of the room.

His silent girlfriend carefully set her glass on the nearby table as she rose to exit. Looking at Grant's stony face, Becca said apologetically, 'He ran out of his medicine yesterday.'

Grant looked at her for a moment, then nodded. 'Medicine was another word for his drug use,' he thought. When he didn't respond, she too, left the room. As he struggled to get himself under control, he stared at the broken glass pieces on the floor. An explosion crash of metal slamming into metal, shattering the late afternoon stillness. Grant ran outside, where he saw his brother's Porsche backing away from his dented Ferrari and with squealing tires, sped down the street. He watched the Porsche disappeared out of sight. Hearing the fracas, several of his neighbors ran to their front yards to see the source of the unusual commotion. His closest neighbor, Dr Afework Amara, crossed his yard to examine Grant's Ferrari. Grant gave a slight wave to Afework's wife, Makeda, in their doorway. She returned the wave before herding their children back into the house. Realizing the source of the commotion had left, the rest of the neighbors returned to their interrupted evening. 'Ian?' Afework asked in his pleasant West African accent.

'Yes. He was not happy that I wouldn't advance him any more money.'

'Was he high again?'

'Actually, I think he was crashing.'

'What are you going to do about it?'

'Get it repaired.'

'Not the car. Your brother.'

Grant sighed, 'I know. It is easier to deal with the car.'

'The neighbors are not happy over this. What if one of their children were out on the street? He could have seriously hurt or killed someone.'

Grant looked up from his car to his friend. 'Is that what you think they thought?'

Afework looked from Grant to his damaged car. 'That is what I thought.' After a few moments of silence, Afework suggested, 'Remember when Makeda had her accident? I'll give you the name of the repair shop. Unless you are considering trading it in.'

'I only had her for barely a year. I can't give her up now.'

Afework nodded in understanding. He took a few steps towards his house when he turned to face his friend, who was still gloomily looking at this car. 'Grant, you realize you have to do something about your brother.'

Depressingly, he looked at the mangled car in the driveway. The car was in front of the garage door. Ian had slammed into the car so hard that the vehicle dented both garage doors. Grant looked at the broken garage doors and hoped the cars on the other side were not damaged as well. He responded, 'I know.'

# Chapter 9

Re-entering the house, Mrs Moore was emerging from the conservatory with the dustpan and broom. 'Thank you, Sylvia.'

'Mr. Priestly, why don't you go to the library until dinner?'

Nodding, Grant went to the library. As he passed the entrance table, he picked up today's mail. Sitting in his favorite chair, he began to rifle through the envelopes. Mrs Moore brought in another glass of ice water. Sighing, she said, 'At times like this, I wish your mother was here. He wouldn't have…' Blinking back tears from her eyes, she turned and left the room.

Pausing for a sip, he knew what Sylvia was about to say. She was his mother's childhood friend and companion.

It has been years since he allowed himself to think about his mother. His parents were married while they were both law students. His mother's field was human rights and civil liberties. His father practiced corporate law. For years, they worked together both as married and business partners until ethical conflicts between the two areas became impossible to reconcile.

Grant remained close to his mother after their parent's divorce. When Barbara was no longer constrained by her husband's business dealings, she began her international legal career in earnest. During his teenage years, Grant read with pride his mother's forays into countries where many of their citizens were denied basic human rights. Grant had barely started his first year of law school when his mother was murdered in Thailand. The Thai government declared the death was a result of a robbery gone bad. The fact that his mother had been investigating and was on the verge of prosecuting an international underage sex trafficking ring was barely mentioned in the local Thai news.

Russell did not agree with many of his ex-wife's principles; nevertheless Grant would always be grateful to his father for working through the governmental red tape to bring her body back for her burial.

Barbara and Sylvia traveled through many hostile and dangerous areas. At those times, Sylvia's husband, Alex, would travel with them. Stepping back from his career as a private investigator, Alex's role was protecting Barbara and Sylvia during their travels. He never let down his guard until that night.

While they were working in Thailand, after a particularly stressful day, Sylvia and Alex decided to relax a bit and visited a local cultural site with Barbara's blessing. Barbara said she wanted to stay in and write up some notes in preparation for the next day's meeting with the head of police.

It was while Sylvia and Alex were out a person or persons unknown broke into their hotel suite and brutally murdered the lone woman. Upon their return to the hotel suite, Sylvia and Alex found Barbara's body. They called both the police and a local physician. Calling a physician was a formality. They knew Barbara could not be alive. Sylvia and Alex never forgave themselves for leaving her.

Upon returning to the United States, Russell hired Sylvia and Alex to maintain the house he had recently purchased for Grant and his younger brother. Ian, living with his father, was rapidly becoming a nightmare. Ian's rebellious behavior did not assimilate well Russell's business ethics. He appreciated the thought of ridding himself of his troublesome younger son while providing for his ex-wife's closest friends. Making two deals at the same time was a productive strategy.

Grant had to admit that Ian was a broken toy. Neither mothering from Sylvia Moore nor discipline from Russell made it past the chip on Ian Priestly's shoulder. The day after Ian's 18th birthday, Ian convinced his father to sponsor an educational trip to Europe to study art. He never lived under the same roof with his family again until moving rent-free in with his Grandmother.

Grant's reflections were interrupted by the ringing of his mobile phone. Not instantly recognizing the number, he answered cautiously, 'Grant Priestly.'

'Grant, this is…..'

'Daniela!' He interrupted with surprise.

'This sounds stupid, but I guess it is too late to hang up now.' She added in a rush. 'My niece is sick, and my brother and his wife decided not to go out and …..'

'Daniela, do you want to go out to dinner?' The aromas of his dinner were drifting through the house. 'I was only planning on having a sandwich tonight.' He lied.

He could hear the relief in her voice. 'Thank you. I would like that. Please, nothing too fancy. I don't have the energy to get dressed up.'

'Tom Wahl's?' he teased, naming the local hamburger place at the local mall.

'hmmm, all right?' she said uncertainly.

'I'm just teasing. I know a place I think you would like. Jeans will be fine. Where do you live?' Daniela gave her address. 'Would thirty minutes be all right with you?' Grant could imagine her smile through the phone. As he closed the mobile, Mrs Moore entered the room. 'Sylvia, I'm going out to dinner. Enjoy the meal. Tell Alex it smells great.'

She looked at Grant for a moment before she nodded her agreement and left the room. In the space of ten minutes, thoughts of his brother receded to the back of his mind. Outside the door, Sylvia heard .'Damn!' Resisting the temptation to re-enter the room, she walked to the kitchen to tell her husband of the interesting change in Grant. As far as the fully cooked dinner was concerned, she knew the baked chicken pasta would taste as good as it smelt. It would not go to waste.

Grant remembered his undrivable car and the inability to get into his garage. Dialling his friend's number, he asked. 'Afework, are you going anywhere tonight? I just made a date and forgot I have no car. Yes, a date with a woman. No, you haven't met her.' After a few seconds of silence, he responded, 'Thanks. I will be over in about five to get the keys.'

# Chapter 10

As she closed her cell phone, Daniela complained to the muted television. 'Why did I do that?!' She smiled at the characters dancing on the screen. Surprisingly, he didn't seem upset that she called. Earlier, when Warren and Bea phoned to say that Emily was ill, she was relieved that she didn't have to babysit. The extra time meant that she could finish the paper tonight, but the research paper was not due until Monday. What other excuse could she think of for not working on it tonight? She preferred to remain enfolded in the emotions she had been experiencing for the last several hours. 'Enfold,' she thought. It is a strange word but it explains exactly what she felt like. She felt wrapped in lovely, warm feelings. The conversation between the two of them was the most interesting she experienced for months. They disagreed on several thoughts, but when they presented their points of view, it didn't seem as if either one was attempting to score imaginary points.

Looking at the clock, 'Damn!' Nine minutes have gone by, and she hadn't even changed yet. Daniela was not surprised when exactly twenty-one minutes later, she heard the doorbell ring. Dragging the brush through her hair, she opened the door.

'Hi, I hope I am not too early.'

'Come in. Are you implying that all women run late?'

'No. No. No.'

She interrupted him with a laugh. 'I am not all women but I am running late.' Ushering him into her living room. She added, 'Two seconds. I just need to put on my boots.' Digging out a pair of ankle boots buried in the shoe pile by the door, she zipped them up while chatting. 'I hope you don't mind that I called. Since you asked me out earlier, I took a chance that you were still free this evening. And I was kind of glad that niece came down with a fever.' Reaching for her jacket from the coat rack, Daniela added guiltily, 'Oh, that sounded horrible. I do love my nieces and nephews. If you haven't changed your mind, I'm ready.' Walking outside, she noticed the deep burgundy BMW. 'Do you have a car for every occasion?'

Grant chuckled. 'No, my car had a slight accident a little bit ago. I borrowed my neighbor's car.'

'Was anyone hurt?'

'No, the car got banged up. It was parked when someone hit it.' Changing the subject, he said. 'Have you ever gone to Swan Inn on Canandaigua Lake?'

On the drive to the restaurant, they chatted about general topics. Surprisingly to both, there were no uncomfortable silences during the trip. The initial topic started with types of foods they enjoyed as children, progressed to the Autumn Event, and then evolved to places they had traveled. Daniela had traveled to several tourist locations within the States. Grant's travels were more extensive than hers and included different parts of the world. It didn't seem as if he was bragging but sharing experiences. The comfortable sensation continued until they returned to her house after dinner and pulled in front of the townhouse.

Daniela was not a virgin by a long shot. When he turned off the car, they sat in silence for a few minutes. Grant began, 'Daniela, I have enjoyed today. I hope you have also.' He picked up her hand, raised it to his lips, and kissed it. 'Please, don't think that I want to stop at your hand, but…?'

'But … it has been a long day. Do you mind postponing…?'

'Until another time?'

Daniela leaned towards Grant, 'May I kiss you?'
'How can a refuse a lovely lady?'
The 100-watt smile appeared again. 'You can't.'

# Chapter 11

On Monday, with a smile pinned on her face that wouldn't go away, Daniela started her morning routine with a quick Alice chat. One look at her face, Alice exclaimed. 'What happened! Who is he? Give me details!'

'No, No, it isn't anything like that,' she lied. 'I just received my course grade, and it was better than I expected.'

'Don't bother giving me that line. The look on your face is not due to any grade.'

Daniela added weakly, 'I did study hard this weekend.' As the phone rang, Daniela dived for it. Alice stared at Daniela's profile as if so was trying to read her friend's mind.

Daniela still felt the warm glow from spending Saturday with Grant. On Sunday, Grant texted, thanking her for an enjoyable day. He said he would not call her because he knew she was working on her paper. He added a smiley emoji. She responded in kind and finished her text with a head-exploding emoji. This morning, she wished him well for tonight. On Saturday, he had told her that he felt obligated to go to one of his friend's daughter's musical recitals. He was not a fan of elementary school musicals, but he was Bette's godfather and felt it was part of his duty to attend. He hoped he would not fall asleep in the middle of it. The messages were not very personal but were fun to send and receive.

For the time being, Daniela did not want to tell anyone about this new … 'What is this?' she thought. 'Friendship? Relationship?' Whatever was happening, she was in for the ride.

********************

Her tightly clenched fist struck the bed pillow for the second time in as many minutes. Her restless body was twisting while endeavoring to find a comfortable position on the bed. This too, failed. Pushing the damp hair out of her eyes, Daniela rolled on her side to watch the red digital numbers on the clock blinking 3:19, then 3:20, then 3:21 with a malicious, evil-clicking tone.

'Damn!' she said out loud as she sat up, disturbing the sleeping animal at her feet. 'Curse all men!' Her newly acquired kitten extended its front paws as he stretched. Tilting her head towards her restless bed partner, the kitten considered whether Daniela was going to get up or not. It would be of interest if Daniela did climb out of bed. Daniela's sister, Lynne, dumped the kitten on her three weeks previously when their Muffin had six unexpected kittens.

Daniela did not want the kitten. Her sister and her nephews overruled her objections and made her feel guilty when she attempted to say no. She named the kitten, Cat. Cat already knew the household routine. She knew that her breakfast would be served shortly if Daniela got out of bed. Daniela sat up and contemplated whether it was worth trying to get more sleep. When Cat realized breakfast was not being immediately served, she curled up and fell back to sleep.

Daniela stared into the shadows of her room, not seeing the shapes of her bedroom furniture. Her thoughts kept circling in her mind. Looking at the clock, which was blinking at 3:28, did not improve her temper. 'This is ridiculous,' Daniela thought as she swung her legs over the side of the bed. The kitten jumped out from among the rumpled blankets to find a more restful place.

It was too late to take a pill that would make her drowsy. If she did, she would be drowsy the following day at work. She didn't think her favorite method of relaxing by soaking in a warm bath would help. Trying to walk quietly in order not to disturb the neighbors on the other side of the walls, Daniela decided maybe hot chocolate could relax her mind enough to get a couple of hours of sleep before her normal 7:00 am wake-up time. Doing a soothing routine task of pouring milk into the saucepan and stirring the cocoa allowed her mind to return to the subject that had been keeping her mind awake lately. Grant Priestly.

It has been a little more than three months since their first day together. They texted nearly every day. 'I feel like a damn forty-one-year-old teenager.' Being seen in public together was brought up by Daniela. As she thought of his name, mental images of him put a smile on her face. 'Damn him!' she said softly. Despite her burning, sleep-filled eyes, peaceful thoughts filled her mind as they wandered over their situation. Initially, it was an acquaintanceship. They met a few times at HMA meetings. The trip to Batavia and dinner (not a date) moved their situation into the beginnings of a fun friendship. Now, what did they have together? A relationship? To say it was a relationship – was the word romantic needed to be added before it. A romantic relationship would be nice. She was not sure she wanted the additional complication. Daniela was content with her life as it was. She was completing her degree. She was not responsible to anyone for her actions. And now what? Her consciousness jerked her back to reality. That thought of 'now what?' has been haunting her for the last couple of weeks and getting stronger daily. Whether she was sleeping or in the middle of a meeting, the words 'Now what?' would flash into her mind without warning. They enjoyed late-night phone conversations. When Daniela first brought up her concerns, he truly understood. 'Now what?' Initially, the question was gentle little thoughts. Recently it is developing into a demand for an answer. It was the lack of an answer which was scaring her. She did not want to be another by-line during a newscast or in a news article or, even worse, a minor note in Grant's life.

Taking the mug and a stack of unopened mail, she sat at the kitchen counter; Daniela tried to deviate her thoughts away from what was keeping her awake. Gosh knows she needs her sleep. Tomorrow's workday was going to be busy and in the evening was her class. She needed her keep her mind focused. Daniela had not had this problem for many years. The problem of not being able to identify her feelings for a man was frustrating. Within a few times of meeting a new man, she knew what form the future relationship would take, whether he would be a friend, acquaintance, lover, or a combination or immediately get rid of him. Finally, she tossed the mail back on the counter and let her mind drift to where it wanted to go as she slipped the warm chocolate drink. After she emptied the mug, she walked into the living room and turned on the 24-hour news channel, hoping that another voice would drive a wedge itself into her circular thoughts. Wrapped up in the sofa blanket, she tried to make herself comfortable.

Daniela watched scenes flash about the war-torn lands where refugees were struggling to survive another day. They made little indents in her thoughts. At any other time, her heart felt empathy for the suffering. Right now, the pictures on the screen are no more realistic than the abstract paintings on her walls. Tonight, Daniela was consumed by her uncertain feelings. She liked Grant a lot – genuinely a lot. Nonetheless, they came from different lifestyles. It didn't take much research to realize she had absolutely nothing in common with either his former wife, his sisters, or any other of his female companions who embellished the society pages. Slowly, the news broadcast was doing what it was supposed to do, numbing her brain so that sleep could overtake her. As she fell deeply into sleep mode, her dreams took over.

Her thoughts turned into non-answerable questions. Is this situation turning into a relationship? Was that the right word? And when? They were barely friends at the time of the HMA Spring Festival Dance. What happened next? They enjoyed each other's company. Talking late at night on the phone. Having sex? No. Not yet. They were careful where they met. Twice at a small diner a distance from the city. The last time was a hidden cove on Lake Ontario that Daniela found twenty years earlier. The early spring weather turning into the summer season with the sounds of the waves gave their twilight stroll a flawless background atmosphere.

When they returned to his car, for a brief moment, Daniela laid her head on his chest as they watched the stars and faraway sparkling of the city lights. The kisses Grant dropped on the top of her head made her long for more of him. When she lifted her face to his, the long, sensuous kiss matched her mood. The warmth of his hands felt the silkiness of her bra and caressed her hardening nipples. With one hand, Daniela unbuttoned his shirt enough to slide her hand against his skin. The softness of his chest hairs only enhanced her sense of touch. Their kiss broke long enough for Grant to whisper, 'I want more of you.' The second kiss was of pure, passionate desire. As their clothing became unfastened, their breaths steamed up the car windows. Daniela did not care how this evening was going to end. She knew she wanted every inch of him.

Tap, tap, tap came on Daniela's side window. A male voice called into the steamed-up car, 'Kids, time to get your parent's car home. The park closes in 15 minutes.' Grant's mouth was pressed against Daniela's shoulder, trying to hold back his laughter when he responded, 'Yes, Sir.' As they heard footsteps crunch away, no longer could they hold back the merriment of the situation.

Daniela spoke first despite remains of the laughter, 'I haven't been caught necking in a car in years.'

Grant was also still laughing as he turned over the engine. 'We better get home before Dad catches us. Laughing, 'I bet I am older than he is.' They pulled out of the cove and drove into the twenty-four-hour Starbucks down the road.' Daniela placed her hand on his hard – what term did they call it in novels? Throbbing member? Whatever it was called, it was appropriate. Looking at Grant, Daniela smiled as she suggested, 'I can take care of it.'

Grant and Daniela's eyes locked for a few seconds. Grant broke eye contact first as he rolled down the back windows and turned the air conditioner on high. 'Dani, my body is hating me right now, but not tonight.' Daniela was shocked at his response. 'Don't look at me like that. I want both of us to share the pleasure – not just me.'

'I am not sure how I am to answer that. I will have to admit that this is the first time I have been turned down.'

'So, I am the first at something,' Grant laughed as he pulled into the drive-thru lane and waited for their turn.

Cupping his face with her hands, Daniela said, 'You are wonderful.' The cars moved slowly up to the ordering menu. The Jag bucket seat made closeness difficult. Fortunately, they could reach over the stick shift console. Then came the disjointed voice, 'May I help you?' Once again, passion was not meant to be as they ordered their coffees.

Parking at Canandaigua city pier, finishing their coffees, they returned to what was started thirty minutes earlier. This time nothing or no one to interrupt them. 'You're a good kisser,' Daniela said softly.

'You are not so bad yourself.' They began to feel the passion in each other mouths.

Daniela raised her eyes briefly to look into his beautiful brown eyes and whispered, 'If you don't stop kissing me, I will not be responsible for my actions.'

'You are testing my limits tonight,' he whispered.

'You're the one who turned on the air-conditioning.' With one last kiss, she sat upright. 'Home, James.'

Laughing at the woman beside him, Grant responded meekly. 'Yes, Ma'am.'

They both understood that sex or lovemaking was in their future. They agreed to keep their relationship to themselves for the time being. People around Daniela knew she was dating someone new. When Paul called her yesterday, he complained good-naturedly that he felt neglected. Daniela told everyone in her life, even her best friend, Cindy, that she was swamped with work, school, and new HMA projects. There wasn't a new man in her life, she lied.

The problem that confronted Daniela was that she knew her time with Grant would come to an end someday. She did not have the least doubt in her mind that this was just a pleasant interlude for the two of them. She could not imagine a future together. Was the pain she would suffer worth the short-term pleasure? She was too tired to worry about it now and fell asleep on the sofa. The alarm woke her three hours later, and she had a smile on her face.

# Chapter 12

Her car windows were rolled down, and the scents of wildflowers along the side of the road were mixed with the aroma of freshly cut grass added to Daniela's feelings of blissful expectation as she drove out to Regency Park. Granted, her classes were becoming more demanding. When her friend and cohort Alicia left Rowe for a new job, it was distressing. Another piece of bad news was that she just had her car in the garage for its pre-annual inspection. It failed. The car needed two new tires. These and other irritants couldn't dent her aura of happiness. Grant and Daniela's relationship was continuing at a comfortable level. Even though the opportunities to meet physically were rare, they cherished the times they could get together. In addition to firmly keeping their relationship just between themselves, the enjoyment of being together was improving. They would use a variety of ways to communicate. During one of their conversation, Daniela said it was like they were in a long-distance relationship even though they lived in the same city.

To Grant, spending time with Daniela was like a hurricane that was surrounding him, and she was the eye of the storm. He felt relaxed and content when he was with her. During their late-night phone conversations, he began to tell her stories about his family, his siblings, and especially his grandmother. They laughed more often when they were together. Grant smiled when he thought of Daniela. He couldn't believe that he was nearly half a century old and enjoying a relationship this much. It was amazing. Both were secretly concerned that if their relationship was exposed, it would change the dynamics.

Daniela smiled when she remembered the time he admitted that he enjoyed being with her. It was after the one rough moment when he asked her to attend a gala event with him. He was surprised when she turned him down. 'Why don't you want to go?'

'I have nothing to wear.'

Laughing, he said, 'That is no problem. You have plenty of time to buy something.'

'I have no money to buy the type of dresses that I would need to wear at one of those events. Not to mention shoes, getting my hair done, and everything else.'

Not considering money in the same light as Daniela, Grant asked. 'Would your feelings be hurt if I gave you the money?'

'Damn right, besides getting very angry at you! Call one of your many lady friends. Any one of them would love to go with you.'

'But I want to go with you.'

'I would ask you why. However, I don't care. You are going out with one of your friends or their 20-year-old daughter and have a perfectly wonderful time. We – I am not going out with you in public together.'

'Why,' asked the perfectly groomed man walking beside her at Niagara Falls wearing a Buffalo Bills baseball cap and blending in with the rest of the tourists, 'Am I that hideous?'

'Horribly Horrendous! And wearing that cap doesn't help much. If you were going to wear a baseball cap, at least make it the Chiefs.' After a slight pause, she added, 'And you know why. Us being together is our secret.' Grant stopped in the path and faced Daniela. He bent to kiss her. The kiss was returned with similar passion. Grant continued to attend the various social events. It was noted that at each event, he escorted a different woman.

Daniela was surprised at the amount of time Grant spent dealing with HMA issues. When she started working a HMA, she knew that he was part of the steering committee and focused on raising funds for the various programs. It did not take long for her to realize that he also physically pitched in with the hands-on tasks. When a group of volunteers offered to give various shelters new coats of paint or worked in the gardens or other tasks, more often than not, Grant was generally one of the volunteers. Because he did not want his activities to be deemed as publicity stunts, rarely did other volunteers know on which occasion he would participate. It was also therapeutic to have some of the guests participate in the upkeep of their lodgings. They began to feel that this was also their home. Not to mention, there was a discovery of a handywoman or two at the house was always a benefit. Sometimes after the volunteers' tasks had been completed, they would go to the local pizzeria. Daniela and Grant laughed at how they could ignore each other so well when they were within the same area. Once, an acquaintance on the HMA committee asked Daniela what Grant had done to upset her. With a straight face, she responded. He just wasn't her type.

It was during one of their rare times alone that Daniela noticed Grant's emotions were at the surface. Most people would not have noticed but Daniela was not most people. When Grant was upset, he became even more distant. Grant and Daniela often told each other stories about their days or families or friends. After the June HMA meeting, Daniela left the room with Samantha to discuss marketing materials. When they separating to go to their respective cars, Daniela's cell started to ring.

'Daniela, are you busy tonight?'

She started to remind Grant that she had her evening class when she hesitated. 'No. I have no specific plans. Why?'

'Do you want to go to the Swan?'

Daniela knew very well that Grant was not interested in the food. 'Fine. Same place? What time?' Quite early in their relationship, Grant and Daniela sometimes agreed to drive separately to one of the local malls and then drive together to their destination.

On the drive out to the Swan Inn, her simple question of how was his grandmother unleashed an eruption. He found out on the previous evening, Ian coerced their Grandmother into giving him ten thousand dollars. He was surprised and then grateful, that Daniela just listened. She did not offer any words of advice or tell him what he should do. After venting his anger and fighting the overwhelming urge to beat his brother to a pulp and then run him over with his car minimized, the pent-up emotions gave way to a clearer mind. They never made it to the Swan Inn. The Swan was substituted for a fast-food restaurant as Grant continued to talk. By the time Grant returned Daniela to her car, his mind was organized enough to devise a plan so that Ian would not be able to take a large sum of money from his grandmother again.

In the days that followed, Grant waited for Daniela to use his confidence as a leverage tool for the hated commitment mania. He had seen it happen repeatedly to his friends, not to mention several times emotional blackmail was used on him. He waited. He knew she would. However, not during the times they spoke on the phone, nor in any of the following texts or at the following HMA meeting, did Daniela say anything about his emotional weakness, which was followed by the outpouring of anger and frustration towards his brother. He couldn't believe that he exposed himself to her like that, and Daniela did not take advantage of it.

When she did not refer to his ranting, Grant began to consider Daniela from another point of view. Most women in his life, including his sisters, had developed a strategy to keep the upper hand in their men's lives. Even his rock-hard father was manipulated by his second wife. Grant knew that Daniela was older than his general companions. Her lifestyle was different than his. Besides the HMA, they had other interests in common. He had not met anyone previously whose company he enjoyed as much.

On a rare evening in which Grant's only plans were to review the budget for 2023, he poured himself a glass of Glenfiddich 18-year-old single malt scotch whiskey. Having the time to relax and enjoy the pleasures of his preferred drink triggered a thought that struck him like a thunderbolt. He has not trusted or confided in someone so much since

Jack. OMG! What if he let Daniela down as much as badly as he had let down Jack?

For several days after Grant's extraordinary thoughts, he did not contact her by either call, email, or text. Daniela missed him. She rationalized that they both had full schedules. It did not take long after knowing Grant when she realized that he kept most of his emotions under lock and key. She felt that his venting was rare, and he needed time to process it. So, she was surprised when she returned to her car after the Business Management class she saw a familiar figure. 'Hi. Have you been waiting long?' she asked, attempting to remain casual.

'It took me a while to find your car.' Hesitantly, Grant asked seriously, 'Do you want to get a cup of coffee?'

Daniela tried not to let the fear in her voice appear, she thought, 'Was this lets-give-each-other-space speech?' 'Sure. We can go to Denny's. Shall we take our cars?'

Grant looked at her curiously. Why was she upset? 'No. We can go in my car unless you are afraid of my driving.' He leaned over and kissed her. 'I have missed you.'

Daniela's emotions did a 180-degree flip. 'I have missed you also. Do you want to go to Denny's?' she asked.

'No, I want to tell you what has been happening. Do you mind if we went for a drive? I do my best thinking while I am driving.'

'Swing around Starbucks. I think we both can use some caffeine.' There were very few cars on the road on a Wednesday night. They drove for two hours. Grant talked non-stop. Daniela asked questions when the story became too complicated. Hidden secrets which came to the surface. At midnight, they stopped at a rest station off the thruway near Elmira. Looking guilty, Grant said, 'I'm sorry I've spoiled your evening.'

'It's not my evening that I am concerned about. We are two hours from Rochester, and I need to be up at 7.'

'You can sleep on the way home,' he offered.

'I have a suggestion. Let's take the day off. I am not above playing a little hooky, and you own your business. We do not need to go back. Believe me, no one is going to steal my car in the parking lot. I can develop a twenty-four-hour stomach bug, and you can have a well-deserved day off. When was the last time you took a day off?'

Grant looked at the woman beside him. Her eyes were red due to lack of sleep, her hair needed a good brushing, and she rarely wore any type of make-up, so why did she look so beautiful to him? 'Dani, let's get a room. I want to spend the rest of the night with you.' Words were not required. Daniela leaned towards him. Her kiss sealed the acceptance.

Grant stopped at the first flashing VACANT sign and booked a room. The queen-sized bed was the focal point of the standard third-rate motel room. Grant grimaced, 'This isn't where I would have preferred.'

'Next time, I will pick the motel.' Daniela walked into his open arms. Pressing against his chest, she didn't want to move. His hand cupped her bottom as he pulled her tighter to him. Her arms wrapped around his neck, lowering his head, lips touching lips. Whatever the room looked like had disappeared. All they noticed was each other.

Eagerly shedding clothes, Grant's toned, trimmed body made her aware of her overweight, frumpy body. Daniela said suddenly, 'I need a shower. I'm grungy.'

Grant grabbed her arm before she could disappear into the bathroom. Pulling her naked body to his slowly, he said gently, 'You are beautiful.'

'I'm fat.'

'You are wonderful. Stay. Please.'

Daniela was a far cry from a virgin, but her overweight, aged body felt as if it was twenty years younger. Naked flesh against naked flesh. They used all their senses to explore each other. The sense of sight - seeing the wave of his hair - the sensual curve of her lips. The sense of hearing - the moans of pleasure as their bodies pressed against each other. The sense of smell. Grant buried his head between the warmth of her breasts, smelling the uniqueness of her skin. The sense of taste. As Daniela ran her tongue up the inside of his thighs, the taste of the sweat on his skin aroused her emotions even more.

Above all, their sense of touch. Feeling every part of each other's body aroused even more sexual desire for each other. The pressure of demanding lips, fingering soft tender skin, hard muscles, or silky hair, along with the scent of desire. The velvety skin of her breasts, the hardness of her nipples when his mouth teased them. Butterfly kisses up his thighs, the manly taste of his – what romance novels call – his engorged member. When the desire to be one consumed them both, he finally thrusted himself inside of her; the explosion of their bodies left each other drained as they remained wrapped around each together. Softly speaking to the head lying on her chest, she said, 'Having an organism is the most selfish thing you can experience.'

Grant's tongue reached out to tease her exposed nipple. 'Give me twenty minutes, and I plan on being selfish again.'

The sun was brightly shining through the muddy-colored curtains by the time they awoke satiated. Every part of their bodies nestled together.

'Thank you.' He whispered in her ear with his arms wrapped around her.

'It was purely my pleasure.' Daniela sighed, 'I hate to be the bearer of bad news, but we can't fall asleep. We both have to call our offices in less than an hour.'

Later, when Grant drove Daniela back to her car, they talked about everything except themselves. Grant laughed, 'Breakfast at Denny's?'

'We are long past breakfast. Lunch?'

Over their meal, Grant asked, 'I have an upcoming dinner. Interested in attending it with me?'

'No.'

'Are you serious?'

'Definitely. I adore being with you. I sincerely hope that this morning is not a one-night, but Darling, neither one of us is ready to go public.'

Taking her hand, 'Dani, I am.'

'Do you mind if we don't for a bit longer?'

When they reached her car, an illegally parked ticket glared at them from the windshield. Grant took the ticket from her and examined it. 'Dani, I'll pay for this.'

She protested but not too much. She was fully aware that her poor checking account was already crying out in pain and agony.

Dropping a kiss on the top of her head, Grant chuckled as he pushed the ticket into his back pants pocket. 'It is cheaper than buying you flowers.'

Daniela gratefully allowed him to win the non-argument. The tightness of her budget did not allow the extra expense of a ticket to rest comfortably within its confines.

Since that day, their relationship become closer. They talked and enjoyed the additional feature of having sex - no! not sex. Once again, what did romance novels call it? Romantic interlude? Making love? How could the term 'making love' be defined? Grant is not the first man in my life, not by a long shot, Daniela thought. How can I possibly explain to my friends what being with Grant is like? Mentally laughing to herself, she attempted to explain to herself the difference between having sex and making love is like…. well, it is like the difference between a shower and a bubble bath. Both will get you clean, but the bath is so much more desirable. She smiled. The attempt to identify the words explaining the difference was not important. Nevertheless, her feelings were extremely important.

# Chapter 13

Laura arrived at the office. Grant was already in his office like usual. But over the last couple of weeks, there has been a change in Grant's attitude. She couldn't identify what it was, but it was there. There were times when she entered his office, and he was doing nothing. Nothing. That was very unlike her work alcoholic boss. She wondered if he was dating someone. Last night, over dinner, Laura discussed it with Oliver. She tried to explain her hunch, 'He seems so distracted lately. I actually had to remind him to review the marketing promos. I have never had to remember him of anything before. He must be in love.'

Oliver laughed at his fiancée's earnestness. 'Laura, he must have had a girlfriend or two in the past.'

She shook her head. 'Not that I have ever heard of. Not since his divorce. He has taken women to different events but no relationships.'

'Gay?'

'Definitely not!' As she considered the sexual orientation of her boss. 'Not that I know of,' she conceded. The matter was soon forgotten as Laura began to discuss their upcoming wedding plans.

Laura thought about the conversation when she entered Grant's office to remind him that Henrik had requested to have a meeting, which was scheduled for this morning. Grant glanced up from his cell phone. 'Was he smiling?' Laura thought. She would give anything to see the message. 'Grant, I just wanted to remind you that Henrik urgently wants to see you. I put it on your calendar for 9:30.'

Grant gave a slight smile, 'Thanks. I did forget.' As Laura turned to leave the office, he added, 'Laura, can you please reschedule all of my appointments for this Friday?'

Laura turned back to face him in astonishment. If Grant stated he was going to close down Priestly Enterprise and head to a desert island, she would not have been more surprised. 'This Friday? Should I reschedule for a few hours or another day? Is there anything wrong?'

'No. Nothing wrong. I am just taking a personal day.' Laura couldn't remember the last time he took a personal day off. The last day he took off was when he had that stomach bug a couple of weeks ago. Asking Grant for any further details was not an option, Laura returned to her desk to do as he requested.

Henrik Wagoner, Priestley Enterpriser's senior corporate lawyer, entered the office precisely at 9:30. Grant greeted him and asked him, 'Coffee?'

'Yes, please. Black.' Laura quickly toward the kitchenette. The coffee maker had not been turned on. Did Grant forget to push the on button? Laura nodded her acknowledgment and left to fulfill the request. The two men sat facing each other. They discussed general business topics until Laura placed their coffees before them and left the office, closing the door behind her.

With no preamble, Henrik stated, 'Grant, we have a situation. You are being blackmailed.'

Grant looked uncomprehending at Henrik. 'Me? For what?'

'Rape, abandonment of the mother and a child born of the rape. The 'go-between' wants 40 million for not spilling details to the media.' As Grant struggled to respond, Henrik continued. 'I have been in correspondence with this person for the last couple of weeks.' Henrik paused to let Grant digest the information. Then he continued, 'At first, I ignored the demand for the lies that they are. Unfortunately, there have been some unsettling details which were sent to me.'

'Henrik, it is all 100% lies and untruths. How can you possibly think such a thing is possible?'

'I don't think it is possible. But we need to sort this out. I just received an ultimatum, which is why we are discussing this now.'

'Why didn't you tell me when this first happened?'

'Do you know how many times people try to shake you down? I receive at least one a week. It is my job to protect you and Priestly Enterprises, not to panic at every ridiculous threat. That is what you pay me for.' Once again, Henrik paused. 'What makes this different is because, for one million dollars, they will send me a copy of the DNA tests which proves you are the father.'

'That is impossible!'

'They are giving me 24 hours to transfer the money, or they will file charges and hold a press conference.'

'I don't know what to say.' At that moment, there was a tap on the office door. Rigidly controlling himself, Grant responded, 'Come in, Laura.'

Laura opened the door and stared at the two men. She never saw Grant look so distraught, not even at his father's death. Nervously, she began, 'Grant, the marketing and sales managers are outside for their 10 am meeting. Should I …?'

Grant interrupted her. 'Laura, give me and Henrik a couple more minutes and let them in ten minutes. Alright?' When Laura closed the door, Grant took a deep breath, 'Henrik, can we discuss this tonight? After work? Would Adele mind if you are late tonight?'

'Of course, we need to thrash this out.'

'Would you mind coming over to my place.'

'7?' Nodding his head in agreement, Grant watched the corporation lawyer and friend leave the office. Breathing deeply before resettling himself at the conference table, Grant pushed the last thirty minutes to the back of his mind. Hoping that his voice was steadier than his nerves, he greeted the team with the next subject on his agenda. 'Good morning, Ladies and Gentlemen. Let's discuss why Wellsbourgh's Homes are perfect for young families.'

Grant felt gratitude for Laura's assistance. She didn't know what had occurred during the first meeting of the day. Nevertheless, her unerring instinct guided him through the day. As Laura dropped off the last bunch of papers on his desk, he looked at the documents sitting neatly ready for his review. He asked, 'Laura, have you recently received any crackpot emails or calls about me?'

Finally, he is going to tell me what had happened, 'In what way? You have had your share of emails and calls about rescuing monies from overseas and penis enlargers,' she tried to install a bit of humor. He raised his eyes to her face. Laura exclaimed. 'Grant, what is wrong? Has something happened to your Grandmother? Your sisters? Ian?'

He shook his head. 'Never mind. Good night, you should be leaving. It's getting late.' After pausing for a moment, Grant added quietly, 'Laura, I will tell you later. Just not right now.'

# Chapter 14

When Henrik left the house, Grant remained seated in the library. He was still reeling from the lies he had been listening to for the past hour. Whoever was framing him had massive amounts of personal information. His mind was screaming, 'This is not right!' As if every step was too much effort, Grant walked to the little used bar in the corner of the library. His hands shook as he poured himself a drink. Sylvia entered the room just as he spilled some of the amber liquid on the ebony countertop. He glanced at his friend and employee. Grant grew up with Sylvia in his life. When his father installed Sylvia and Alex in the house, initially, he had difficulty being close to a person who was so much a part of his mother's life.

As time passed, it was no longer an employer/employee relationship. When Alex and Sylvia decided not to have children, Barbara's children became their children. The girls were married with families. Whenever they returned to Rochester, they visited Sylvia and Alex as well. Sylvia insisted that Grant call her Mrs Moore in front of any non-family visitors. Sylvia and Alex were quite content with their lives and resided in a comfortable apartment off the kitchen wing of the house.

'Since you did not eat much of dinner, do you want…?' Her words died in mid-sentence when he turned to face her. 'Grant, what is wrong?' she demanded.

'Sylvia, could you please ask Alex to come in here? I need to talk to both of you.'

Without a moment hesitation, Sylvia crossed the room and dialed the kitchen's extension. When Alex arrived, Grant began speaking in a husky voice. 'Earlier today, Henrik Wagoner told me that I am a target of a blackmailer.' He paused for a moment to gather his thoughts. 'The criminal,' he said the word with pain, 'has threatened to expose me as a rapist or at least a molester of at least one underage girl. I – I got one of them pregnant, then abandoned both the girl, and after she gave birth to a child, I threatened them if she told anyone.'

'What! Who is saying that?' exclaimed the Moores together. Sylvia added, 'How can anyone say that of you!'

'Obviously, they can. They seem to know quite a bit about me.'

'Who?' demanded Alex.

'That's the point,' Grant said. Talking over his problem with two of the people who had known him for more than thirty years was steadying his nerves more than the drink in his hand. 'There is a third party involved because the victim is afraid of me! The go-between will not say who she is because of my threats against her and the child. The blackmailer won't even give a date of when this happened for the same reason. As 'proof of evidence,' they will give me a copy of the DNA test results for the cost of one million dollars. One million to 'verify' and I use that term loosely that I have fathered the child.'

Sylvia shook her head as Alex asked, 'How much are they demanding in total?'

'Forty million.' Stunned silence filled the room. Reflecting on his conversation with Henrik, Grant added, 'One million to see the DNA evidence, which needs to be paid in 48 hours. Then the balance after that.'

'If you paid the million, how is the money to be paid?'

'Bitcoin.'

'I have heard of Bitcoin, but what is it? I mean, what country issues Bitcoin currency?'

Alex took his wife's hand in his as he explained, 'Bitcoin is a type of cryptocurrency. Digital currency.'

'Imaginary money? Do stores accept it?'

'No. Bitcoins aren't like a dollar bill that you can handle. It is usually used by criminals and operates outside most countries to avoid regulations that banks have to follow. Criminals can use cryptocurrencies instead of the formal banking system to move large sums of money which entails a potentially lower risk of being detected by law enforcement or the traditional financial institutions which are required to submit suspicious transaction reports. But Bitcoins can be a perfectly legal method of investment.'

Sylvia said suspiciously to her husband, 'How do you know about this?'

Nodding toward Grant, who was contemplating the bottom of his drink, he said, 'We can talk about Bitcoins later.'

'What are you going to do?' Sylvia asked Grant.

'I don't know. Henrik received the initial email from a phone account that is no longer working. Since then, messages have been received via text using disposable SIM cards. Henrik hired a private investigator last week when he realized that these were not crank requests. This detective has not affiliated with Priestly Enterprise or any of its cases. Naturally, we were warned not to contact police or an investigating agency. Going to the police is risky because leakage is possible. Henrik thought it would be safer if we could find the blackmailer ourselves. Priestly corporation has several investigators on the books, but Henrik thinks that one of them could be the go-between because of the knowledge this guy has on me.'

Taking a deep breath, he asked the Moores, 'I have no timeframe, but can you recall anyone taking special interest in me? A delivery person? A repairman? It could be anytime or anyone.' The Moores looked at each other and then at Grant. He leaned back in the chair, his drink forgotten. 'What an impossible question. This supposed rape could have happened nine months ago or thirty years ago. It could have happened here or any of the dozens of places I have stayed at.'

Sylvia and Alex stood up. Sylvia walked over to Grant and placed her hand on his shoulder. 'Grant, Alex, and I are here for you; we always will be.' Grant looked at his mother's best friend. No words were needed. He patted the comforting hand. Responding to the nod toward the door by his wife, Alex stood and said, 'If we think of anything, we will let you know. But at the moment, nothing comes to mind.' The Moores left Grant to his thoughts.

Grant glanced at the grandfather's clock ticking steadily against the opposite wall. It was only 9:30. Less than three hours since Henrik came over with the blackmailers' demands. Only twelve hours when he first heard the threat. Grant felt helpless. He wanted to call the blackmailers' bluff. He knew that once the allegations were made, even if or when they were proven false, it could affect his life and the business. It wasn't fair, he repeated to himself. It isn't fair.

Grant was restless, but he didn't have the energy to move. As he watched the minute hand move, a random thought flashed into his mind. Daniela would be leaving the college campus in a few minutes. Her classes were over at 9:30. As his mind formed the name, her smiling image appeared. He was still intrigued as to why he enjoyed her company, but now he couldn't imagine her not being in his life.

With two younger sisters, Grant had been in the company of females from an early age. 'What an adorable little boy' were the first words he remembered hearing from his parent's friends, especially the wives. As he reached his teenage years, both his female schoolmates and his sisters' girls' friends paid quite a bit of attention to him. When he started noticing the opposite sex, he perceived that they had noticed him in return. At fifteen, he learned that he had choices in the manner in which he could deal with the opposite sex.

His parents gave him contradicting advice when he suffered the pain of his first teenage teary-eyed break-up. The love of his life decided that the captain of the football team was more to her style. Even though Jack spent time telling him what a slut she was and he was better without her, Grant was heartbroken because he thought he was in love with her.

His father's advice was to use them before they use you. Everything comes at a cost. His mother explained to him that it would do him well to consider the other person's motivations. The reason why someone acts the way they do is sometimes more important than the act itself.

Grant reflected on his early relationships. As rich, attractive teenage boys, he and Jack indulged in fun and games when they could find them.

His ex-wife, Helene, had been the daughter of one of his father's friends. Their marriage started so promising. Even Jack liked Helene; she was sweet, kind, and loving. They had similar backgrounds and knew a lot of the same friends. He thought their relationship would stand the test of time. Unlike many marriages they had observed, rarely did they have angry words or dramatic fights. It was a comfortable, loving lifestyle. Three years into the marriage, Helene announced to him she was filing for a divorce. Grant shook his head to dislodge the memory. She told him she only married him because her family demanded she should. She was in love and wanted to be with Fatima. She couldn't continue the lie. Men had never interested her romantically. She and Grant would always be friends.

His mind continued in its circular contemplation. Who were the other females he had been involved with? Who did he get pregnant? Was there a pregnancy? Was this all a scam? By whom? The clock chiming at the quarter of an hour brought him back to the here and now. It was 9:45. Impulsively, he picked up his cell phone and dialed.

'Hello?' questioned the voice. Then, in the next second, he heard, 'Grant! Hi! Wait one second. I am just getting to the car.' As he heard a metal thump, he imagined the books and phone being put on the car roof as she unlocked the car door. After a couple of moments, he heard, 'Okay, I'm in the car. Bluetooth is on. I'm here.' Then, a sigh. 'It is nice to hear your voice. How are you doing?'

Grant leaned back in his chair, thinking how normal she sounded. 'I'm fine. I was thinking of you and decided to take a chance on giving you a call. How was your class?'

Daniela was pleased that Grant was calling but mystified. Their relationship was progressing nicely. There were multiple phone calls and fun texts. Every several weeks, they would go out for an occasional meal.

More often, they order a takeout and have it delivered to various hotel rooms. For different reasons, they decided to keep their relationship under the radar. Daniela continued to see the relationship as being short-term. Tired of the expectations that he should remarry, Grant was enjoying the stimulating and, at the same time, relaxing atmosphere with Daniela.

'I had the management strategy class tonight, and it was really interesting. We examined the psychological situation between management and ' her voice trailed off. Daniela knew he wasn't listening when silence greeted her unfinished sentence. His mannerism was the opposite of their previous evening's chat. 'What's wrong, Grant?'

'No. Nothing. Yes. I mean, no, I just wanted to hear your voice.'

'Hmmmmm. There is something wrong. Tell me, or I'll drive straight to your house and shake it out of you!' They both knew it was an empty threat.

Grant admitted, 'It was a little bit of a rough day.'

'Sweetie, I know it is late, but I will be home in about 5 minutes. It is a weeknight, and we both have to work tomorrow, but if it is easier to talk in person instead of on the phone, come over. I will make hot chocolate. I will kick you out at midnight before I turn into a pumpkin.'

It was on the tip of his tongue to say 'no,' but he said, 'Hot chocolate sounds good. See you in a few.'

Minutes later, the hot chocolate was ready to be poured when her phone rang at the same time. There was a knock on the door. Turning off the stove, Daniela picked up her phone and recognized Greg's number. She answered the phone and heard the second knock on the door. Opening the door, she put her finger to her lips for Grant and answered Greg's greeting.

'Darling, how are you? How are the wife and kiddies?' Daniela motioned Grant into the living room, who sat at one end of her sofa while she returned to the kitchen. 'Greg, I just got home from school. What can I help you with?' Trying not to look like he was eavesdropping, Grant heard, 'I am sorry, I can't do Friday. I have plans.' Silence then, 'When do I have time for anyone new? Take your wife out. She would appreciate it. Not a problem. I understand. Chat later.'

Dropping the phone on the kitchen counter, Daniela returned to the living room with two mugs of hot chocolate. Momently forgetting the problem which had plagued him for the last twelve hours, Grant asked, 'Is that your boyfriend?'

Daniela placed her mug on the coffee table as she sat on the opposite end of the sofa. She laughed as she propped herself in the corner. 'Grant, I am far too old to have BOYfriends. Yes, Greg is a gentleman friend of mine. Greg and I met when he was separated from his wife. They got back together, but we have remained friends.'

'….. and lovers?' Why was he feeling jealous?

Ignoring the question, she turned to face Grant directly and asked, 'There is something wrong. What is going on?'

Grant struggled for a moment. Should he pursue the answer to his question? Deciding he didn't want to know the answer, he hesitantly began with the morning meeting with Henrik. He didn't realize until he was finished that Daniela had moved closer. He could feel the warmth of her hand covering his. He concluded, 'Of course, it is blackmail. But what if ……'

'Do you think that you are capable of forcing a woman or girl to have sex with you?'

'No. I don't mean that. I mean – what if I am a father?'

'Wow!'

'What do you mean?'

'I mean, you are not thinking clearly. You are being shaken down. Oh my god…. ' Daniela exclaimed when she looked at his face. Pulling him close to her, Daniela held him as his arms wrapped around her. The silence was not interrupted until Grant released his death grip.

Resting against the sofa back, Grant complained. 'This is the most uncomfortable piece of furniture I ever sat in.'

Picking up the cold liquid, she asked, 'Darling, let's change the subject from insulting my sofa to how they know so much about you. Someone needs to know about you and or your business to know how much to blackmail you for?'

'What?'

'I mean, why ask for forty million? Why not a hundred million or only ten million?'

'After everything this person says he has on me, you are curious about the blackmail amount?'

'You said that a private investigator is working on this? What does he say?'

'I don't know. Henrik hired him.'

Placing her mug back on the table, she faced Grant, 'Sweetie, I know this has thrown you for a loop, but something about this doesn't seem right.'

'Don't you understand, Dani, this could …'

'No, it won't.'

'You don't understand.'

Losing her patience, Daniela interrupted. 'Stop and think for a minute. Forty million is a lot of money, but it won't cause your company to fold. If this lie is exposed, the worst part will be to your ego being battered. Also, who could have got a hold of your DNA to use as a comparison to this child?'

Angry that she was not offering more sympathy, he countered, 'How do you know how much the company can handle?'

'Because I am not an idiot. Even though Priestly is a private company, little research shows that the company can hold that much of a debt loss. And it is well known that your father worked on the 'cash is king' principle. That is something he spoke about all the time. And besides the garage full of cars, you are careful with your money.'

Glaring at Daniela, secretly glad he could get mad at something tangible, he snapped, 'Have you been spying on me?'

'Of course, I have,' she said calmly, 'You could be a rapist.'

Grant looked at her in disbelief. After a moment, he started laughing. Daniela handed him back his cold mug of chocolate. 'Let's look at the sensibly. In less than twenty-four hours, you have been told you are a scum bag, you are a father, and your company will be destroyed… maybe… because of your actions, someone wants to ruin any positive influence you may have done. And before you can sort through all this you have a deadline of forty-eight hours to decide about a million dollars? Even though a million dollars won't break you, it still is a chunk of change. Does that about cover it?' She paused before adding, 'Have you molested or raped anyone? Male? Female? Young? Old? Something from the animal kingdom?'

'Daniela, this is serious!'

'I know it is. However, it seems that someone, or a group of someones, is trying to keep you from thinking clearly. What does that lawyer… Henry… say?

He automatically corrected her, 'Henrik? He says to pay the million, let's see what they have.'

'What do you think?'

Daniela's voice and her closeness allowed Grant to relax for the first time since his nightmare began. 'I can't think.' Stifling a yawn, he added unnecessarily. 'I'm exhausted.'

'Do you want to break our rule? You can spend the night.'

Smiling for the first time. 'Would we sleep?'

She agreed, with a returned smile, and taking the mug from his hand as she stood up, pulling him to his feet, she walked with him to the door. 'You're right. Go home, Darling. Get some sleep. Your instincts are good. You will know what to do.'

At the door, he leaned over and kissed her. 'I would like to stay, but I need to go home. The deadline is at noon, and there is a lot to think about.' He added, 'You're wonderful.' As they kissed good night, Daniela almost said those fatal words, 'I love you.'

When Grant got back into his car, he turned his phone back on. Puzzled, he noticed that he had four voicemail messages, all within the last thirty minutes. His equilibrium, which had returned while he was at Daniela's, was gone. Two of the voicemails were from his stepmother, Tiffany, making some unintelligent demands that he could not cope with at the moment. One voicemail message from Ian. The last voicemail from Henrik asking if a decision had been made. Returning to the security of his house, Grant forced himself to go to bed without responding to any of the messages. With prescription assistance, he was able to get a few hours of sleep before heading into the office.

He knew he would make the payment. Hopefully, the private investigator could find who was behind these lies.

# Part 2 – Hell's Fire

*If you are going through hell, keep going. – Winston Churchill*

# Chapter 15

Grant heard his half-sister's voice before he reached the kitchen. Leaning against the kitchen doorframe, he observed Rachel chatting at the table with Sylvia while Alex was standing at the stove, smiling into the saucepan he was stirring.

'What are you doing here, Brat?' He affectionally greeted her. 'Does your mother know where you are? Why aren't you at school?' Referring to the outrageously expensive school in Switzerland that Rachel had been attending for the last five years. He seated himself at the table.

'Hi, Gee. I came home….. hmmm … four days ago. The school had to shut down for a couple of weeks because EVERYONE there was getting the flu or it could be covid, but whatever it is, they didn't want us around. I can tell you the Princess is not happy to have me at home. She tried to get them to keep me there, but they wouldn't. Right now, Princess is sleeping in the arms of Prince Valium, which is why I was able to sneak out and visit you.' Rachel imitated her mother's whining voice. 'She had such a stressful time today.'

Grant smiled as Alex attempted to turn his snort of laughter into an unconvincing cough. It was left to Sylvia to remonstrate the teenager. 'Miss Rachel, you shouldn't speak about your mother like that.'

Spacing her next words like a royal proclamation, Rachel said distinctly, 'She is not my mother.' Laughing at the shocked faces around her, she added, 'I have been told to call her 'Tiffany.' She looks far too young to have a daughter my age.' Rachel grabbed another Oreo off the plate Sylvia had placed between the two of them. 'Mmmm, I miss these. Sy, when are the Girl Scout cookies being sold? I love the Peanut Butter ones… no, I like the Carmel deLites the best.'

Grant opened a cupboard door. 'It seems that we have only the S'mores left.' He tossed an unopened box on the table.

As she ripped open the box, Rachel correctly guessed, 'Barbara?'

'And this year Heather is also in the Girl Scouts.' Grant's nieces kept the family supplied with Girl Scout Cookies. 'Didn't your mother buy any?'

Are you kidding? I swear Princess thinks that she can gain weight by smelling them. She already says that I am fat as a pig.'

Sylvia and Alex looked at each other as Rachel reached into the box for another S'mores. Rachel was a slenderly built teenager with a curtain of golden blonde hair. If it wasn't for her impish grin and her sparkling blue eyes, she could be taken for one of the many porcelain dolls that filled her bedroom.

'Your mother likes to be called Princess?' Grant questioned.

'Dammit, Yes!' Rachel said disgustedly. 'And it is my fault. I called her Princess because she acts like she is so perfect, and we are all her slaves. I know she thinks her shits come out as chocolate ice cream. Once I called her Princess in front of her snooty friends. And what happened - that stupid Mabel asked why I called her that. Do you know what the bitch said? She told them that I once saw her dressed up, and I told her that she looked like a fairy princess and I have called her Princess ever since then. I can't believe the lies she tells, AND as I was leaving the room, she said… she actually had the balls to say to her friends…. she thinks the best word I can call her is 'mommy'! If I called her 'mommy,' she would stab me to death with one of her fingernail files.' Rachel ended dramatically.

Quickly changing the subject, Grant asked, 'How did you get here?'

'I drove.'

Knowing his sister's age, he said quite unnecessarily, 'You are not old enough to drive.'

'I know but I have been driving the Princess' car since last summer.'

'What if you were caught?'

She beamed her smile at him, 'I'm a good driver. I haven't been stopped.'

Trying to be stern, Grant started, 'Young lady, you know you shouldn't drive, especially Prin… I mean your mother's car.' He dropped his paternal act when everyone started laughing at his slip of the tongue.

Standing up, he asked, 'Rach, have you had dinner yet?'

'No. But you haven't asked why I am here.'

'To see me.'

Rachel pulled from her purse a folded note and placed it on the table. 'Since I have been home, Princess has been on the phone to Mariah and Eleanor,' referring to her half-sisters, 'and especially to Ian.' Looking confused, she asked, 'What's going on? She never talks to the family. She only talks to you because you control the money. And I think I heard her talking to Helene.'

'My ex-wife?' Grant asked in disbelief. He reached for the folder paper. Opening it, he exclaimed as he looked at it. The note reminded him of ramson notes in old-fashion crime novels. The note had words made from individual letters cut out of newspapers. Glued on the note was a newspaper picture of Grant and his stepmother, which was taken at a charity event last year. The letter said, 'How would the rapist Grant Priestly look on the news? Are you innocent?'

'Fuck!' said Grant forgetting his surroundings as he threw the note back on the table. The Moores scanned the content.

'You swore!' exclaimed his sister. She was more shocked at her brother's use of profanity than the content of the note.

Quickly gathering his thoughts, Grant asked his sister, 'Do you want to go out and grab something to eat?' When she nodded, Grant said, 'I was coming to the kitchen to say I was going out to eat tonight. Sorry, Alex, for the late notice.'

'No problem, Sir.'

'Let's go, Rach. Sylvia and Alex, can you do me a favor?' Taking a house key off his key chain, he handed it to Sylvia. 'Can you drive Tiffany's car back to her house? If the Brat is right, Tiffany will still be sleeping. Just drop the car key someplace in the house where she can find it.'

He then addressed Rachel sternly, 'Rachel, promise me while you are here, and if you want to go anywhere - call an Uber or me. I promise you that I will make arrangements – no questions asked. I will have you picked up or dropped off at any place – and at any time that you want.' He turned his little sister to face him directly. Putting his hands on her shoulder, he tilted her face up to look at him. 'Promise me you will call, okay? I don't want anything to happen to you.' He released her and gave her a quick hug. 'On your next birthday, if your mother doesn't arrange to take you to get your permit, I will drive you down to the DMV myself. Do I have your promise?'

In her life, where love seemed to be in short supply, she loved her brother. She put her arms around his waist, squeezing him, she said gruffly. 'I promise.'

As she released her brother, she scooped up her jacket and purse. In her normal voice, she asked, 'Where are we going?' As they walked toward the kitchen door leading to the garage, the Moores heard, 'I'm starving.'

# Chapter 16

The majority of Rochester's residents considered September to be the premier month of the year. It is the time of the year when the heat of the summer transforms into a patchwork of luscious red, orange, and yellow foliage of autumn. The colors of the countryside would not be at their peak for a couple of more weeks. The weather was warm and nonpareil for driving. When Grant and Rachel entered the garage, she asked, 'Can we take the Jag?' He agreed. She added with total innocence, 'Can I drive?'

Good-naturedly, Grant responded, 'No.'

Twilight was beginning to descend upon the community. As they drove along the country roads, Rachel barely noticed the variety of colors.

Looking shyly at her brother, she said, 'Are you going to tell me what is going on?'

'Yes, I will, but you have to promise me what we talk about tonight will be our secret. You cannot tell any of your friends or…' he paused a moment before adding, 'Your mother.'

Derisively, she said. 'Me telling Princess anything. No way.' As a new thought occurred to her, she questioned him excitedly. 'Are you gay? Is that your secret?'

Taking his eyes off the road for a moment, he looked at his sister and repeated. 'Am I gay?'

'Sure. I mean, why not? You haven't been dating anyone since…..'

He interrupted her, 'No, I'm not gay?'

Warming up to a new theme, she asked, 'Are you a spy? I mean, you can travel anywhere, and spies are always….'

Laughing at Rachel's imagination, he interrupted her again. 'No, I am not a spy. You were closer with your first comment,' before she could interrupt, he rushed to say, 'I'm not gay! I have a girlfriend. We've been dating off and on for about the last six months.'

Confused, Rachel needed clarification. 'Why is she a secret? Is she married?' Or as another new thought occurred to her, 'Is SHE a spy?' Without stopping for a breath, she changed the topic, 'Why are they saying you are a rapist?'

'I'm being blackmailed. You are going to meet her now. Her name is Daniela.'

'The blackmailer's name is Daniela?!'

Grant reached over and squeezed his sister's hand reassuringly. 'No, Sweetie. Two different topics. I'm being blackmailed by someone who is threatening to tell the news that I am a rapist. They say they have evidence.' He added, 'I'm not, you know.'

'I know that. Who is Daniela? Is she pretty? Have I met her before? Why are you keeping her a secret?'

'I met Daniela at one of my business meetings. I think she is very beautiful. Not your mother beautiful, and ' he added softly, 'she is wonderful.'

Rachel stared at her brother's profile. Her parents had little time in their busy lives for her. She barely turned ten years old when an elite girls' school was discovered for her in Switzerland. Rachel always felt like an ornament for her mother. She knew her father loved her but when she would receive too much attention from him, Tiffany would have the nanny remove the child from the room.

Grant was more like her father's than Russell had ever been. He always seemed to be able to make time for her until she went away to Maryvale Academy for Young Ladies. Before she went to boarding school, Rachel could always count on her big brother to attend her school and sports functions. He taught her how to kick a soccer ball while her parents were vacationing in Hawaii. She had so much fun learning how to play. Grant solicited the household staff – both live-in and day workers - to join in and take the different positions on the field. Who would have guessed Alex Moore was so good at the game?

The last year at her local school, St Joseph's held their annual fathers and daughters' dance. Grant escorted her. Unfortunately, said her mother, the school activity conflicted with an important gala event for which her parents had a prior commitment.

On her ninth birthday, her parents were traveling in Japan. They told Rachel's nanny to take her to Darien Lake with a few of her friends. The plan was never put into effect. After Nanny Delphine picked up Crystal and Lisa Anne to go to the park, she said they had to stop at Grant's house for his birthday gift to her. Rachel couldn't believe her eyes.

Grant's backyard had been turned into a circus ground. There was a huge tent and ringleader, complete with a red jacket and top hat. The circus included a show with clowns, two baby elephants, and ponies. The children could ride with the elephant or ponies or both. Most of her class and young people from the neighborhood were there. Food vendors had set up booths for hotdogs, hamburgers, cotton candy, and every type of circus food she could imagine. Her birthday cake was shaped like a unicorn. As each child left, Grant gave them a small gift. In reality, Laura gave out the gifts. She had been dressed up as Cinderella and helped manage the energetic children. Everyone had so much fun! Even the parents who attended!

Most people who saw Grant and Rachel together thought that they were father and daughter because of the 30-year age gap. It used to bother Rachel but now she didn't correct them. She often pretended that Grant was her dad. Maybe someday Laura could be her mom.

Rachel could always count on Grant to listen to her. When her parents flew with her to the new boarding school, they stayed for the required twenty-four hours and then left as soon as they could. Her father had to get back to work, and her mother had so many meetings which required her attendance. These were the reasons they gave her. Rachel remembered she was so homesick the first few weeks after being enrolled at Maryvale Academy. The first night they were able to call their families, she called her mother. Her mother told her to grow up and stop acting like a baby. Her mother reprimanded her and told her if she kept crying like that, none of the other girls would want to be her friend. The next time she was allowed to phone her family, she dialed Grant's number. When he answered, she couldn't help herself. She tried to explain her feelings. No, the other girls weren't mean. It wasn't that. She tried not to cry like her mother told her.

It was with the best luck in the world Grant happened to have some upcoming business dealings close to the school. She was so grateful when he visited her. His business engagements last for nearly two weeks. There was an evening when he picked her up after her classes, and they went out for dinner. Another time, he included in the dinner invitation three other girls whom Rachel had been chatting with and hoped would become her friends. Another time, with the approval of the school, he located an American-style pizza place and ordered a variety of pizzas for the girls in her residence hall. The very, very, VERY best time was when Grant received special permission to take her and her new friend, Stephanie; to London for the weekend as her tenth birthday present. The highlight of the weekend was seeing Beauty and the Beast at the Prince of Wales Theatre, then they ate at a fancy restaurant. By the time, Grant's business meetings were over and he needed to return to the States, Rachel was able to manage her homesickness and became her cheerful self again.

Rachel cherished the times when Sylvia would make her awesome salt caramel and chocolate fudge and send them to her school. Sylvia would always include several of Rachel's favorite magazines. Five years later, Rachel knew that the magazine subscriptions could have been sent directly to her school, but being ten years old, opening packages every couple of weeks meant a lot to her.

Glancing again at her brother driving, she saw him smiling. Even when Grant was married to Helene, Rachel never remembered him smiling when he said her name. Not like he did when he said, 'Daniela.' Carefully exploring this side of her brother, she asked cautiously, 'Why are you keeping Daniela a secret?' The concept that her brother was a rapist was so far removed from her knowledge of him that she disregarded the accusation.

'Well, you know how your mother likes publicly?'

'Sure, Princess won't leave the house unless she knows a camera will be there.' Unnecessarily, she added, 'Or she will have Patricia call the press.' Grant was aware that if the publicity was not up to Tiffany's standards, she would have her social secretary call one of their favorite society reporters.

'Whatever.' Grant dismissed his stepmother's activities. 'Daniela is not like that at all. She – we - like a little bit of privacy.'

'Oh,' remarked Rachel, attempting to process the information that not all people liked to be the center of attention. She had not confronted that concept previously.

As they pulled up in front of the Swan Inn, Grant noticed Daniela's car was already parked. Entering the restaurant, Grant greeted the hostess as he walked to where Daniela was seated. She was looking out the window, watching the stars twinkling reflectively on the mirror-smooth lake. She glanced up when Grant touched her shoulder. 'Hello, Darling.' Then she noticed the teenager behind him. Instantly she said, 'Rachel, how are you?'

Defensively, Rachel said, 'You know who I am?'

'Of course. When I read the flu epidemic was closing businesses and schools in Switzerland, I was wondering if one of them would be yours. When did you get home?' The waitress approached to take their drink order. Daniela said, 'Diet Coke, please.'

Rachel interrupted, 'I don't want a coke. I would prefer to have a glass of wine,' addressed the waitress, intending to appear sophisticated.

Before Grant interrupted with a lecture about underage drinking, Daniela said, with a straight face to the waitress. 'I have changed my mind; I will have your special Rose wine, and this young lady will have a diet coke. Grant, the usual?' He glared at her and nodded.

When the waitress left, Daniela said, 'We will exchange drinks when the waitress comes back. You don't want to get the waitress in trouble for serving a person under eighteen alcohol.' Rachel's beaming smile almost made up for the confused frown from Grant.

Confidentially, Rachel leaned across the table towards Daniela, 'Where are the bathrooms?'

Rachel barely left the tables when Grant hissed at her. 'What do you think you are doing?'

Patting the clenched fist on the table, 'Darling, do you think that the Swan never had an underage kid wanting alcohol before? I noticed a few weeks ago a technique the staff uses to prevent meltdowns by having two special drinks. It is just one step up from a Roy Rogers and a Shirley Temple. They are called Special Rose Wine or a Jack Daniels Round-Up. It's a soft drink with about one tablespoon of either Rose Wine or Jack Daniels. Hopefully, before the kids discovered how diluted their drinks are, they have reached their drinking age.'

Grant laughed as he leaned over the table to kiss Daniela, 'You are wonderful.'

'Get a room.' Rachel said as she returned to the table.

After their meal order was taken, Grant pulled out the crumple note Rachel had brought to his house earlier. After reading a few words. Daniela asked Grant, 'Where did you get this?'

Rachel responded instead of her brother, 'Maybe today or possibly yesterday. Princess has been on the phone with everyone except Gee.'

Correctly identifying who 'Gee' and 'Princess' were, Daniela asked, 'Everyone?'

'Yep, Mariah, Eleanor, Ian, Helene. I don't know who else. Those are the only names I heard. Of course, Princess never tells me anything.'

Grant took over the conversation. Keeping their voices low and changing topics when a waiter or waitress approached, Rachel learned of the events that had been transpiring over the last two weeks. 'Wow!'

Rachel said at the end. 'Wow!' she repeated. 'So, did you pay the million?' Grant nodded. 'And the DNA evidence?'

'I haven't received anything yet.'

Rachel asked hopefully, 'Maybe it was a one-time scam?'

Daniela also waited for Grant's answer. 'We received a text this morning. The proof will be here shortly. Whatever 'shortly' means.' Grant pulled out a note of his own. 'Henrik received this picture this morning. It was sent to Henrik's phone. Naturally, the SIM card is untraceable.' The subject was a close-up showing the back of a head. The hair color was similar to Grant's hair coloring. Whether the head belonged to a boy or girl, teenager or toddler, was not identifiable. The caption read 'Look Familiar?'

Rachel made a derision sound, 'That could be anybody.'

Looking at his sister's golden hair, he laughed, 'I couldn't be you.' Their food was set in front of them and the topic was changing when Rachel's phone became demanding with its rings.

Even though Daniela could not identify the individual words, she could hear the unmistakable angry tones across the table.

'I'm with Grant.' Pause. 'He took me out to dinner. You were sleeping.' Longer Pause. 'I took a taxi.' They both watched the girl's face crumble as the yelling continued. Finally, Grant held out his hand for his sister's phone. She handed it to him silently. Daniela got up and motioned Rachel to join her outside on the deck surrounding the restaurant. As soon as they exited the building, Rachel exclaimed in a voice throbbing with tears, 'Bitch!' Daniela put her arm around the distressed teenager's shoulders.

A few minutes later, Grant joined them. 'Rachel, your mother is not feeling well.'

'You mean drunk.'

Grant let the comment go without challenging it. 'Do you want to spend the night at my house? I am sure Sylvia can find you some pjs?' With her head bent, her hair became a screen hiding her face, and she nodded slightly 'Yes.' Hoping to change the subject to reduce emotions, he asked, 'Does anyone want dessert?' Silently over their heads, Daniela shook her head 'no.'

'Sorry, Darling. I can't. I have to be getting home.'

Reaching the cars, Grant gave Daniela a light kiss and squeezed her hand. 'Thanks,' he whispered. She blew him a kiss as she slid in behind the driver's wheel.

Rachel stared straight ahead as they started the ride home. For the first ten miles, the only sound was tire meeting the road, then taking a deep breath, she said, 'I like Daniela.'

'Me, too.'

'Why didn't the two of you drive out together? Does she live out her?'

'No, she lives in Rochester off of University Avenue. She was out this way, and we just met here.' Pausing for a second, Grant asked. 'Are you okay, Sweetie?'

'I hate it when she drinks.' Taking a ragged breath, she asked, 'Gee, how much trouble are you in with this blackmail stuff?'

'Don't worry about it, Rach. I have managed worse things than this.'

'Have you really?'

Laughing at her earnestness, he admitted, 'Not really, but there is always a first time. Did I tell you Laura is getting married?'

'Really? I always thought you two would get together.'

# Chapter 17

Grant grabbed his phone from the bedside table before the first ring finished. 'How is she?' Daniela asked.

'Sylvia got her settled in. Tomorrow she is going to take her out shopping. Unfortunately, all her friends here are at school. Dani, that little girl has had such a rough life. Dad didn't have much time for her and Tiffany…. well, Tiffany has always been a bully. I don't think I ever saw Tiffany hug her or even hold her when she was little.' Daniela listened quietly. 'Rachel is such a sweet little girl. She had always been surrounded by adults. She deserves a family. Not a drunk for a mother and bunch of servants.'

'Darling, she has you.'

'It's not the same.'

Daniela thought of her crazy family and its members and agreed. 'Grant, we may have a slight problem. The Moores don't know I exist. I mean, I am sure they suspect that you have someone, but they don't know officially. Do you think Rachel will tell Sylvia?'

Sitting up in the bed, he glanced at the clock. 'You're right. It's too late to tell them now. I tell them tomorrow morning before I leave for work. Are you sure you are okay with me telling them?'

'If Rachel was not involved, I would have preferred to keep it quiet for a bit longer. We can trust the Moores, can't we? With everything going on, let's keep 'us' low-key. Is that okay with you?'

'Of course. Until this blackmail thing is settled, I would rather keep you out of it.' There was a slight pause, and then he added, 'Dani, thanks for everything tonight.

'Rachel is a great little girl.'

'She would hate you for calling her a little girl.' A chuckle was heard over the line. Grant had been considering his next words over the last couple of days. 'Dani, you don't have to respond but…but...'

'I love you too.'

'You're not going to run in the opposite direction because I said I love you.'

'Not this time. We'll talk tomorrow, all right?'

'Of course. Sleep well, Darling.

# Chapter 18

Before he left for work the next morning, Grant spoke to Sylvia about his relationship with Daniela. As suspected, Sylvia thought he may have been involved with someone. Rachel was still sleeping when she recounted the conversation to her husband. In the end, she added, 'I'm glad that it was only a girlfriend.' As a good husband should, Alex agreed with his wife.

Neither Grant nor Daniela had a spare moment to meet up over the following week. Priestly Enterprises seemed to have progressed into overdrive with new and current projects. Only a handful of people knew what was going on regarding the blackmail situation. Grant had to restrain himself from picking up the phone and checking with Henrik to see if he had any further updates. Henrik repeatedly told Grant not to take this situation personally because whoever was behind the scheme wanted money, not to attack him personally. If it was personal, the story would be all over the news by now. After hearing Henrik's entirely plausible, and most likely explanation, for the third time, Grant erupted. He was a person, and he did feel it personally. For the first time, people in the offices around the CEO's office heard an enraged, furious voice.

The thundering sounds reminded several of the older employees of his father but not Grant. Grant didn't get angry.'

The eruption was never heard again. Once, Grant suggested to Henrik that he wanted to hear what the private investigator had discovered from the man himself. Henrik thought it might not be a good idea. Henrik was attempting to minimize the connections between the investigator and Priestlys. To most of Priestly's employees, after his outburst, Grant just seemed a little more distant than usual.

Naturally, Laura was in her boss' confidence. For the third morning in a row, she brought Grant's coffee to the office and set it on his desk. Grant looked at the mug and then at Laura. 'Can you please close the door?' When she did what she was asked. Grant pointed to the chair, and she sat down. 'Laura, you have to stop doing this?'

She didn't attempt to plead ignorance. 'Grant, this is horrible, and I can't do anything else to help.'

Taking a sip from the mug, he said, 'Thanks, but you are going to have the office gossiping. You barely bring me coffee in five years and now it has been three days in a row. They are going to think we are having an affair.'

She gave a short laugh. She knew words to that effect were already being whispered. 'What can I do?'

He looked at her, 'Frankly, I don't know until we receive the DNA proof.' He started laughing at a thought that occurred to him. 'Maybe get me another cup of coffee tomorrow.'

'What? I mean….' Began his confused assistant.

'If the gossipers are speculating about us, let's give them something really to talk about and do it in style. But no, I was only kidding. We don't want that type of gossip with your wedding….'

Unknowingly, Grant had hit upon a subject that she needed to discuss with her boss. Looking down at her fingers, nervously fidgeting in her lap, she asked hesitantly, 'Can I have my job back?'

He looked confused at Laura. Two weeks ago, they had begun the interviewing process for someone to fill her soon-to-be vacant position. 'What do you mean? What about the wedding? Oliver?'

'Last week, Oliver's father had a massive heart attack.'

Why didn't you tell me? Where is Oliver? Did he fly back to England, and why didn't you go with him?' He knew that Oliver's family had already considered Laura their daughter.

'You were going through so much; it didn't feel right for me to leave here.'

Grant was touched by her loyalty. He asked gently, 'Your wedding plans?'

'We are rescheduling the wedding for a year from now next August. Same plans, just different dates. We want Papa Martin to be healthy for the wedding. I had sent out notifications to the guests. Most of the wedding plans were easily rearranged.' With an attempt at humor, she added, 'The wedding dress will still be in style. I am just hoping none of the bridesmaids get pregnant.'

Grant was sorry for Laura's postponement of her wedding plans but secretly relieved that she would be staying. He disliked the thought of breaking in a new assistant. 'I didn't receive a notification about the change of your wedding plans?'

'I wanted to tell you in person. It isn't totally bad. Oliver received an offer to stay on after he graduated in June. He applied for a research grant, not expecting to receive it. The announcement was made a couple of weeks ago that his project would be one of the recipients. It was the next day, his mother called about his father. When it was confirmed that we received the grant, we decided to stay in Rochester for an additional year. The research will be a massive help when he begins his Ph.D. program.'

Trying to read her demeanor, he asked, 'Are you okay?'

'A lot has happened in a short time. My brain is still trying to work through this.' Taking a deep breath, Laura was back into her business persona again. 'I better get back to my desk, and you need to finish your proposals.'

Changing the topic, he said, 'Rachel is heading back to Switzerland tomorrow. She will be staying with her friend, Mia Thyes, and her family until Maryvale opens. I don't know how Tiffany got them to agree. Hopefully, Maryvale will open within the next week or two. I wanted to have lunch with her today at Barneys. She loves that place. The poor girl hasn't had much fun since she arrived. Most of her friends around here have been at school. But I need to review this proposal and return it to Diane before 2. Could you entertain her for a bit? Looking guilty, he said, 'I know I shouldn't ask you…..'

Rachel was well known to the Priestlys' employees ever since her father brought the angelic blonde bundle of baby charm to the firm. Initially, it was Tiffany and the little girl who visited the office to have lunch with Russell. As Rachel grew older, Tiffany dropped out of the boring luncheons. At least a couple times a month, the adored daughter would meet her father at lunchtime. They would either eat in the employees' canteen or at a local restaurant. Both Russell and Rachel looked forward to the luncheons. When Grant's schedule allowed, he joined them.

The older employees watched Rachel progress from an infant to a toddler. They saw her holding her formidable father's hand while making her first tiny steps into a little girl with missing teeth as she smiled. Reaching her pre-teenage years, she was all arms and legs as she headed to her fancy school. Whereas Russell felt discontented with his wife, he only experienced delight in being with the daughter of his later years. The twenty-five years between his two sets of children did not bother him in the least.

The last time Rachel was at Priestly Building was just weeks before the Covid shutdown. Rachel attended the annual Christmas luncheon for all the employees. The employees who remember her earlier visits remarked on how the skinny pre-teen metamorphosed into a beautiful, self-assured young lady. Rachel had a smile for everyone and remembered many of their names. Russell was proud of his teenage daughter. The resemblance between Tiffany and Rachel was striking. The dark coloring of the Priestlys did not influence Rachel. Rachel inherited the Priestly family's height. Tiffany was barely five foot four. Rachel was nearly three inches taller than her mother.

Laura knew of the special relationship between the little girl and her protective older brother. Despite being the apple of her father's eye, Rachel grew up in an adult household. Both Tiffany and Russell had an active social life. Tiffany's artificial inflation of her social status made her decide that most of Rachel's friends were unworthy of Priestly's attention. Since this was how pampered Tiffany was raised by her adoring parents, she deemed it only appropriate for her daughter.

Grant remembered his mother taking time from her busy schedule to participate in a variety of activities with him and his three siblings. Whether she would take the kids camping or amusement parks or just local activities, Barbara encouraged them to try new activities, from artistic creativity to physical challenges. When he saw his little half-sister, he was reminded of the difference between the laughing, wrestling, and happy household to Rachel's perfectly rigid doll house upbringing. There were many times, Grant would ask Laura's opinion for a birthday or special occasion gift. Grant would generally begin the conversation with Laura with, 'You used to be a little girl.'

Laura did not know the entire story between the two households; however the pictures of Grant and his siblings' family parties were in stark sharp contrast to the second Priestly family's perfectly posed pictures.

Laura hadn't risen from the chair to return to her office when they heard Rachel's voice. She was chatting with the various employees on the way to her brother's office.

'Darn, she's here! Laura, you know.... '

Laughing, Laura held her hand out for the corporate petty cash charge card. 'Where are we meeting for lunch?'

'Barneys at 1:30. I promised Rach a new phone.'

'What's the limit?'

'I don't want to mortgage the house.'

'Right.' Just at that moment, there was a knock on the opened door and without waiting for an answer, Rachel walked in. Laura was the first to speak. 'Rachel, I like the new haircut. Looks good on you.' Holding up the charge card, she added. 'Your brother is being boring today. I understand you are looking for a new phone. I've got the card. Let's go shopping. We'll meet him for lunch later.'

'Barneys?'

'Of course! Where else would we go?'

Happily accepting the change of plans, Rachel hugged her brother. 'Bro, I'm glad you can't come. You are such a tightwad.' Over Rachel's head, Laura gave her boss a wink.

'Brat, don't spend all my money.' Grant played along. 'See you in a couple of hours.'

# Chapter 19

While Grant was managing his affairs, Daniela was wrapping up her last few classes before the end of the semester. It was a rare Saturday afternoon that Daniela and Cindy were able to go to Starbucks for some catch-up time. By the time Daniela had pulled her car into the one remaining parking space and located her friend, she was ready for the skinny, medium-sized latte sitting in front of her empty place. 'Have you been waiting long?'

'Not really. As soon as the kids got into Jeff's car, I was out of there in a flash. Okay, Lady, nearly four weeks! What is going on?' Looking at her friend's guilty face. 'OMG, please don't say you got back together with Steve.'

'No, no, no. It's not like that.' Then, thinking, she started smiling, 'Maybe a little like that.'

'Okay, spill the details!'

'Actually, I can't.'

'Is the new guy married? That hasn't stopped you before.'

'Cindy, he isn't married. He is the most wonderful man that I have ever met.'

Suspiciously, Cindy asked, 'Then why can't you tell me about him?'

'I know this sounds strange… but I can't.'

Cindy knew her friend long enough to remember several of her outlandish romantic interludes, which they laughed about when the adventures were over. At the time, Cindy laughed at them, but some of the escapades seemed downright dangerous. There were times that she was afraid that she would find a story in the news that her friend's body would be found in some remote place. Seriously, she asked, 'Dani, is there anything I should be worried about?'

Daniela was touched by her friend's concern. 'Not at all.' Cindy was looking more upset with each passing moment. Cindy couldn't remember a time when Daniela didn't share her romantic life with her. 'Look, Cindy, we can't talk here. Let's get some takeaway cups and go to the Pond.'

Because Daniela's car was cleaner of the two vehicles, they drove over in her car. They chatted about inconsequently topics until they reached Mendon Pond Park. Seating on the bench, they barely took note of the few runners circling the pond. Only the ducks seemed interested in the two women. When they realized neither Cindy nor Daniela had food for them, they also lost interest and waddled away. Cindy listened in total silence as Daniela explained her latest romance. Daniela purposely did not mention anything about the blackmail attempt.

At the end of the story, Daniela finished the last swallow of her cold coffee. 'So, what do you think?'

'I think you should write a book.'

Daniela gave a short laugh. Her various friends had said for years that she should write a book about different aspects of her life – especially the juicy parts. 'Now, Cindy, you cannot tell anyone. Not even Tony. I am deadly serious. Please promise me!'

'I mean, Dani, Grant Priestly. Wow!'

'Look, if this relationship goes the distance, we will let the world know, but not at the moment. We like being together. I don't want to be put in a reporter's lens. You know how many skeletons I have in my closet. What do you think it would be like when one of the Town and Country Top 50 Bachelors is interested in me? Oh, com'mon, Cindy, you understand, don't you? I mean, he has dated models and even royalty. Then there is me. Please, Cindy, this is extremely important. The only reason I told you is because I know you are worried.'

'I will promise I won't even tell Tony. But there seems to be more to this that you're not telling me. Is there any more?'

'Yes. A little. I can't tell you because it is someone else secret, not mine.'

'Dani, I am 100% trusting you, but if you need anything, let me know. Well, you are dating number 14 of the hottest men in New York State. Once again, Wow! Okay, let's change the subject to… hmmm… shall we say the other men in your life? What is Steve up to? Is he still trying to get back with you? I mean, he can't if you are dating….' She added lamely, 'someone else.'

'Well, I finally changed all the locks in the house,' and laughing, she added, 'No, that didn't stop him. But Caroline did.'

'Who is Caroline?'

'Someone who started in the human resource department. She took Janice's job. I was transiting the HMA stuff to her… well, Caroline was with me when Steve sent flowers to the office about four or five weeks ago. I knew Steve needed to pursue someone else besides me. While Caroline admired the flowers, it flashed in my mind. A plan!!!' They both started laughing. Cindy knew her friend well enough that she always had a plan in addition to a couple of backup plans. 'I showed Steve the company photo of Caroline and asked if he wanted to meet her. The rest was easy. Caroline and I went out to lunch. Guess who we happen to meet – Steve. According to both Steve and Caroline individually, things are looking promising.'

'Paul?'

'I told Paul that I was in love. He told me to touch base with him again when I stopped being in love. He is the last of great cynics.'

'Greg?'

'Him and his ever-growing family are moving to Ohio at the end of next month for his new job.'

In humorous disbelief, Cindy asked, 'You mean you only have one man in your life?'

Taking Cindy's gentle mocking in the manner it was meant, she responded, 'It looks like it.'

# Chapter 20

When Daniela picked up her ringing phone, without any preamble, Grant blurted out, 'We just got it.'

In her best business voice, she responded, 'Good Afternoon, Mrs Jerome. And what will be the next step?'

'DNA tests are being analyzed now.

'Where are you now?' Daniela partially covered her mouth as she whispered in the phone.

'In the office. Just getting ready to go into a meeting. Henrik stopped in a couple of minutes ago. I just wanted to let you know.' Grant finished apprehensively. Darn if he knew why he wanted to share everything with Daniela. 'Are you free tonight?'

'Okay, yes. Thank you.' Being in an open-planned office meant that every conversation was public property. As she hung up her phone, Alicia's replacement, Brian, questioned her, 'Was that the Abbott's rep?' The office plan incorporated a series of working pods arranged throughout the office. Each pod consisted of two pine-color individual desks facing the two other individual desks. The configuration created a pod of four desks and, generally, eight listening ears. As intended, private phone conversations were discouraged.

With a straight face, Daniela blatantly lied, 'No, that was Claire from Charles.' She named a customer rep who she knew was on maternity leave. Rowe's had an unofficial rule that cell phones could not be used during work hours. Using Grant's middle name if they needed to talk during the day, they could make arrangements if their two schedules happen to sync up.

In the short time that Brian was employed by Rowe, she did not trust him. He seemed to feel the only method for advancement was to enhance himself to the detriment of other employees. So far, it seemed to work. Brian had been securing Ken as his new best friend. Daniela thought that if he worked as hard at his job as being Ken's best buddy, everyone would be happier. She was not surprised when she found out that she was not the only person in the department with similar feelings.

Daniela laughed when Brian managed to convince Ken that he would be a better representative than Daniela at the HMA functions. It only took a couple of HMA meetings for Brian to realize that there was real work involved. Daniela had to thank Grant for playing a part in her plan. One evening she explained to Grant her distrust of Brian. At the next meeting, Grant requested Brian's assistance over the weekend at one of the shelters. Initially, Brian took Grant's request as a personal acknowledgment of Brian's social adeptness.

However, he was horrified when he found out that he was expected to work with the guests at the shelter. On Monday, Ken and Brian had a meeting. Hence, Caroline was assigned as Rowe's representative. Grant also assisted Daniela with another situation – Steve. Grant gave Caroline a small but visible role at the upcoming Spring Ball. The major requirement was Caroline's obligation to attend the event. Daniela suggested Caroline to request Steve to be her escort. Previously, Caroline had told her that her boyfriend had left her, and she was sure that Caroline did not have time to become interested in another man. And knowing Steve as well as she did, Caroline's damsel-in-distress attitude would appeal to Steve's ego.

Since Daniela did not attend the event, she listened to Grant's description with unholy glee. To Grant's unexpressed relief, Steve was no longer in the picture.

Returning to the current situation, Daniela asked Brian, 'I am assuming you have the stats for the meeting in about…. Hmmmm, fifteen minutes.' When Brian began complaining, she knew he had not done what he was assigned. Earlier in the day, Daniela compiled the information required. She would have helped Brian with the report if he had asked, but he didn't. Unobtrusively, Daniela slid the stats amongst the other documents for the meeting. Brian may have thought because he was fifteen years younger than her with a college degree that he was all that. She stole a look at him as he attempted to locate the various documents necessary. Slightly shaking her head at the self-centered man-child across from her, she understood how Brian and Ken became such good friends so fast.

After the satisfying departmental meeting, Daniela returned to her desk. Scanning her emails, she saw an out-of-place message. It was from Rachel. She knew that Grant gave Rachel her email and phone details but this was the first time Rachel contacted her. The message scared her. All it said was G in danger. R

Daniela's eyes were glued to the screen for a few seconds. Without a moment's hesitation, Daniela quickly printed out the message. Then, she deleted the message from her inbox folder. For additional security, she also deleted it from her delete folder. She knew she couldn't delete it totally from the computer system, but the message would be harder to locate. Daniela needed to contact Grant.

'Oh Drat!' She had loudly in the office. Brian looked up at her. 'I forgot my dentist appointment was for today. I mark it for next week.'

Brian mockingly said, 'The perfect Daniela made a mistake.' She ignored him as she grabbed her purse and headed toward Ken's office. A few minutes later, she drove to a supermarket parking lot where she thought the chances would be slim to none that someone from Rowe would see her. She called Grant.

When he picked up his phone, she blurted out, 'Darling, I need to see you now… like right away.'

Grant was about to make a flippant remark, but he stopped when he heard the urgency in her voice. 'Dani, I am heading to a meeting. What's going on?'

'Rachel just emailed me. It sounds bad.'

'Does she need money or something?'

'Grant, I have never asked you for anything… we need to talk as soon as possible. Alone.'

Checking his watch, he said, 'Dani, I can meet you at Canal Park. Near the pavilion in about fifteen minutes. Is that okay?' Without realizing it, Daniela began nodding yes. 'Dani? Dani? Are you there?'

Her voice quivered as she laughed, 'Sorry you couldn't hear me nodding. Yes, in fifteen.'

As she drove through her favorite coffee house and ordered their coffee, Daniela tried to figure out a reason for the message from Rachel. If it indeed was from Rachel. What if it was just a joke? Fifteen minutes later, Daniela got in Grant's car. She handed him his coffee and then gave him the printed message. He looked from the note to her. Without a moment of hesitation, he began dialing Rachel's number.

Grant started to say, 'Rac….'

His little sister's voice whispered, 'Danger!!!' and the phone went dead. Grant dialed again. No answer. Repeat dial. No answer.

Trying to keep control of her voice, Daniela asked. 'Grant?'

Grant was furiously entering numbers on his phone. 'I don't know what is going on!'

'Joke?' Dani whispered.

'Oh God, I hope it is!!!' Changing the tone of his voice, he spoke on the phone, 'Hey Tiffany, yes, I'm sorry for interrupting your manicure. Have you talked to Rachel? Yes, I know she is an ungrateful child. I agree no one would believe you are a mother of a teenager.' Daniela marveled at how Grant was maintaining a calm voice. 'I agree that sounds like the perfect summer camp for her. Have you talked to her about it?' Listening to about thirty seconds, he concluded the conversation with, 'I'll talk to her.'

Putting his head on the steering wheel in despair, he said, 'What is going on?' Sitting up again, he looked at Daniela as he told her about the whispered word. Then he had an idea. 'I'm calling the school.' Dialling the school, he spoke to the headmistress. 'I see. Thank you.'

For a few seconds, silence reigned in the car. 'Rachel is with a group that is spending a long weekend in Prague visiting some Cathedral. I asked them to have her give me a call. Family emergency.'

'Grant, what is going on?'

'I have no idea!' The thought of his little sister in any type of dangerous situation filled him with panic. The idea that he was in danger was far removed from his current thought process. Daniela placed her hand over the white knuckles wrapped around the steering wheel. Various plans were running through his mind. She didn't interrupt the silence. Before he started the car, he handed the phone to Daniela. 'Keep dialing Rachel's number. You are going to meet the Moores.' It was not a request.

As she began to speed dial Rachel's number, 'Are we leaving my car here? What if it gets impounded?'

'I'll buy you a new one. Any answer?'

'No. It just rings and then goes into voicemail. Am I going back to work today?'

Grant looked at her for a moment. 'Dani…?'

'Darling, I am not bothered. I want to be with you until we find Rachel.'

# Chapter 21

As Grant explained to the Moores what had transpired, Daniela continued to dial Rachel's phone. Then a thought occurred to Daniela, 'Grant, if I keep calling, all I'm doing is filling up her voicemail box. Do you want me to call the school again?'

'Okay. That's a good idea.' She speed-dialled the number and handed the phone to Grant. Once again, they were disappointed when the school phone went into its answering machine. Daniela called her office. Explained that her car had been hit on the way back from the dentist. No, she did not know how long it would be.

Grant took a deep breath before he called his office. 'Laura, I have a bit of a problem here. What meetings are scheduled for the rest of the day?' After listening for a while, he said, 'Move Donny's to next Friday. Take the PR and Lydia's meetings and move them to Wednesday. Now I need your help. No questions, please. Do you have my personal email password? Good. I am at home sick – you don't know for how long. I am in no shape to talk to anyone. Check my personal emails. If you see anything suspicious, let Sylvia know. I can't tell you.' After a pause, he added, 'Laura, absolutely no one under any circumstances is to contact me until I contact you. Understand?'

Closing his cell phone, he looked at Alex, Sylvia, and Daniela. 'Call the local police?' Sylvia asked.

Grant grimaced, 'And tell them what? A spoiled, rich girl is pulling a prank?' As he marshaled his thoughts, he asked, 'Dani, is there anything at your house that you need?'

'Just the cat that needs to be fed, but I can have my sister do that. What are you thinking?'

'I need to contact Rachel.'

'Grant, she said YOU are in danger.'

'I can take care of myself. She is only fifteen.' A sob escaped from Sylvia.

'Shouldn't her mother be told?' Alex asked.

Sylvia said bitterly, 'That bitch could care less about her daughter.'

Daniela's eyes widen at the hatred in her voice. She also quickly realized it was because of the love Sylvia had for the girl. 'Grant, what is your plan?'

'Dani, I want you to stay here. Don't let anyone know where you are. Anything clothes you need, anything – order it online and have it delivered. Can you please stay here until…?' his voice trailed off.

'Of course. I'm glad it is Friday. Oh wait, it's my night at Roselyn. Should I tell them I'm sick?' Grant nodded yes. 'If necessary, I will call work over the weekend and say my grandmother kicked the bucket.' She surveyed the Moores' startled faces. She added reasonably. 'It's okay, she won't mind. She passed away when I was five.'

The weak chuckles broke the tension in the kitchen. 'Okay,' Grant smiled at his love. 'I hope this will be solved by tomorrow. I'm flying to Switzerland as soon as I can get out of here and talk to Rachel. Alex, after you take me to the airport, can you get Daniela's car and park it at the training station or wherever for a week? Sylvia, they know you at Maryvale. Try calling them every once in a while. Not too often to make them suspicious. I don't want them to call Tiffany. I'm not sure what is happening, but I want to keep her out of it as much as possible for a while. Dani, keep trying to get in touch with Rachel. I'm leaving my phone with you. Since I will be out of touch during the flight, she may try and call me. We know she has your details. Drat, she emailed you at your work. Did she also email you at your home email address?'

'I don't know. I didn't check.' Pulling up her emails on her phone, she said, 'Yes, she did. She emailed both of them! Oh no, what if she emails me at work and I am not there.'

'Who can access your emails at work?'

'Ken and, of course, the IT department.'

'I hope no one will check your emails for the next couple of days. We will deal with your work later. I am hoping if she contacted you once, she would contact you again. I'm going to take the other phone; I will give you the number to reach me as soon as you hear from her.'

Sylvia asked, 'Do you want me to book flights?'

'No, it will take too long. I'm chartering a flight.' Standing up from the table, Grant reached out his hand for Daniela. 'Time to see the rest of the house. Alex, I will be ready in 30 minutes.'

They walked hand in hand to the library. Ruefully, Grant said, 'This is not the way I wanted to introduce you to the house.' Before she could reply, his lips were on hers. Their arms were around each other. He needed her closeness after the last few hours of uncertainty.

'I am scared, Grant.'

He kissed the top of her head. 'I know. I'm terrified. What if she is mixed up because of this blackmail mess? Whoever is behind this knows a lot about me.'

'They wouldn't hurt her. What would be the benefit?'

'Dani, you are asking questions. I have absolutely no answers.' Releasing her, he became all business again. 'Here is the number for my other phone.' Then he began dialing again as he walked to his bedroom to throw a few items into an overnight bag.

# Chapter 22

Twenty-eight minutes later, Sylvia and Daniela were alone in the kitchen. 'Miss Daniela, if you want to go into the lounge, there is a television in there. I will make up the yellow room for you… unless you were …'

Daniela interrupted Sylvia, 'It's just Dani, please. Let me stay in here for a bit if you don't mind. I.. I… I would rather not be alone.'

Despite Grant's obvious fondness for this girl, Sylvia was prepared to dislike her. No one was good enough for him. However, with this one, well, time will tell. Unbending slightly, Sylvia said, 'We haven't had a chance to eat lunch yet. Do you want something to eat?'

In the silence of the kitchen, Daniela's stomach decided to make its opinion known. After the growling stopped, she said meekly, 'Yes, please.'

'Dining Room or here.'

'Here, please.'

As Sylvia warmed up the soup and made them sandwiches, she said, 'When we get done with lunch, I'll show you the rest of the house.'

# Chapter 23

For the next three days, the house was tense with anticipation. The Moores and Daniela barely spoke about anything beyond the current situation. Ten hours after Grant left the house, they received a message with the one word, 'Here.' As Daniela predicted, Rachel's number no longer accepted voicemail messages. The headmistress icily told Sylvia that when the chaperone contacted them, she would relay the message. The headmistress seems to imply since she was neither Rachel's mother nor her guardian, Sylvia's request would receive low priority.

The first evening after dinner, Daniela went into the lavish living room to watch the television. After sitting through some silly sitcom, she couldn't remain by herself. Wandering back into the kitchen, she found the Moores playing Scrabble. They included her in the next game. The Moores were usually actively keeping the house on Oakfield Street running smoothly. However, they could barely manage any activity except watching the silent phones.

All three of them had hoped that within several hours, Grant would call them with some news. At first, they hoped for good news. After a sleepless night, they wanted to hear any information from Grant. Several times, one of them would suggest calling Grant. They didn't. Hours passed then two days had elapsed with no updates. The eternal games of Scrabbling became the focus of their attention.

Over game five, Sylvia began telling stories about the Priestly children. At first, as a friend of the family and now, as living with Grant. Over game twelve, stories were being to be shared about Rachel. She was the apple of everyone's eye except her mother. During game twenty, Sylvia told her first story about her best friend, Barbara. Alex was working outside during this game. As Sylvia talked, the game was briefly forgotten. When Sylvia tightly closed her eyes to prevent the tears from flowing, Daniela got up from the table to make a cup of coffee for the two of them. Sitting the cup in front of her, Sylvia took a napkin and dabbed her eyes dry. 'Grant is so much like his mother. I don't know how I could live if something happens to either Grant,' she paused for a moment, then added with a sob, 'or Rachel.'

In response to her thoughts, a banging started on the front door, interrupting her confidence. Sharing a look at the sudden noise, Sylvia said, 'No one is to know that you are here. Quick, go into my apartment.' She pushed Daniela towards the apartment which she and Alex called home. She wiped her eyes one last time on the dish towel before answering the door.

Glancing at the doorbell security camera, she opened the door to Ian and, silently trailing after him, Becca. 'Where is Grant!' Ian demanded when Sylvia had barely opened the door.

'He is not here.'

'Bullshit. All of his cars are in the garage. Tell him I am upset. Very upset.' Ian walked through the house straight to the bar in the conservatory.

'He is not here.' Sylvia insisted. Just as Ian was opening his mouth, Alex walked into the library.

'Where is he?' Ian handed a glass of amber liquid to Becca while pouring a tumbler for himself. 'He didn't drive.'

'No, Sir.' Alex replied.

'Where did he go? When will he be back?'

'I am sorry, but I can't answer for his whereabouts because I don't know where he is. Nor do I know when he is returning except he was going out for dinner.'

'Well, you can tell me where you dropped him off.'

'Of course. I understand his first appointment was with Gilmore.' Naming an exclusive men's clothing store in Pittsford.

'Well, I will just wait right here until he comes home.'

Unflappable, Alex replied, 'Of course, make yourself comfortable.'

'I will.' After a moment's pause, he said, 'I'm hungry. What's for dinner?'

Sylvia noticed that he never included his girlfriend in any of the conversations. Alex responded smoothly. 'Since Mr Priestly was eating out, we were going to make our meal of fried liver with onions.'

'Fried liver!'

'Yes, Sir. With onions and spinach.'

'Bullshit. That isn't what my brother would eat.'

'No, Sir. But he is not eating in tonight.'

Getting bored with the conversation, Ian slammed his glass on the bar top. 'Tell His Highness, I want to see him as soon as he gets home,' and strode from the room. Becca set her glass down and quietly followed behind.

As soon as Alex made sure that they had left, they started laughing at the scene while telling Daniela what had happened. The ring of the phone Grant gave Daniela echoed in the kitchen; it stopped the conversation dead. She was it snatch up. With relief, she heard Grant's voice. 'Darling, I will explain everything later. Give the phone to Alex.'

Alex didn't say a word into the phone except 'Okay.' As he hung up the phone, he faced the waiting women. 'He wants me to pick him up at an airstrip in Albany.'

'Albany?' they responded. Sylvia exclaimed, 'That is almost two hours away. Did he say anything about Miss Rachel?'

Alex said, 'No. He only said to pick him up. We will find out what happened when he gets home.'

Both women were watching television in the Moores' quarters, lost in their thoughts. Hearing the car pulling into the drive, they waited to hear the garage door locked. Looking at each other, they rushed to the back kitchen door. The door opened, and Grant walked in, looking for Daniela. He held out his arms, and she was in them.

A kiss was barely exchanged when there was pounding on the front door.

Only Grant didn't seem surprised. Quickly, he shoved his overnight bag and coat in Daniela's arms. 'Get her into your apartment. Stay there.' Sylvia grabbed Daniela's hand and pulled her through the doorway they just used moments before. 'Take your time answering the door,' Alex walked slowly to the front door.

Alex opened the door. He feigned surprise at three police cars in front of the house, and two of Rochester's finest were at the door. Alex assumed that at least four more policemen were covering the other entrances into the house.

Grant joined them in the hallway within minutes. 'Gentlemen, may I help you?'

'We would like to ask you a few questions regarding your half-sister, Miss Rachel Priestly.'

He looked calmly at them. 'Of course, come in.'

Grant led the officers into the library and closed the door firmly between them and Alex.

Two hours later, in handcuffs, Grant was walked into the hallway escorted by the officers. Alex and Sylvia watched them moving towards the front door. Grant said calmly, 'Sylvia, call Laura. Have her get a hold of Adrian. Naturally have her reschedule everything on my calendar for the next few days.'

# Part III

*Life Begins on the Other Side of Despair … –Jean-Paul Sartre*

# Chapter 24

Headlines were massive. *Local Businessman Arrested for Murder*. Stories ranged from physiological analysis of why Grant Priestly 'allegedly' committed the homicide to gory details of Miss Rachel Priestly's murder. The victim's mother was seen everywhere. Continuously dabbing tears from her eyes, she gave her opinion regarding suspicions of her stepson's unnatural favoritism for her beloved innocent daughter.

Since Rachel's body was found in The Czech Republic, the crime became an international feature within a blink of an eye. Both professional and freelance media news reporters camped out on Oakfield Street. Every member of the Priestly family and a significant number of friends and acquaintances were hounded for their opinions and, hopefully, a quote or two. Grant Priestly's sisters, Mariah and Eleanor's reactions were concise and to the point. They were heartbroken over the death of their little sister. Nevertheless, they believed in their brother's total innocence. They firmly believed that the truth would be discovered, all charges would be dropped, and there would be justice for Rachel. Once their spokespersons made their statements, no further comments were given.

Every neighbor on Oakfield Street was accosted as soon as they stepped out of their houses. Police surrounded the Priestly house and began removing boxes, which included electronic devices such as laptops, desk computers, tablets, security cameras, and various cell phones. After searching the Moore's residence, the investigating officers did not enter the house again. At least one police car always remained in front of the house after red paint was thrown on the front of the house and the word 'murder' painted on the garage doors. Since Grant's arrest, he was deluged with threats.

Meanwhile, Ian, looking biker chic before the cameras, claimed that he had suspicions for years that his brother was grooming young girls, regardless of the fact of how much Grant and Priestly Enterprises attempted to cover it up. As an afterthought, he threw in that Grant was being blackmailed and why. These comments brought up more questions than answers.

Priestly Enterprises experienced immediate repercussions from the allegations. Clients disassociated themselves from Priestly Enterprises. Very few people wanted to see their law firm's CEO in the news for murder.

The day after his arrest, Grant stood before the judge for his plea. Of course, it was not guilty. Despite Adrian King's most persuasive arguments, the court decided that Grant could not be released on bail – even under house arrest. The prosecuting attorney stated that a substantial amount of evidence had been obtained against him. With the Priestly's wealth and connections, even if he surrendered his passport, there could be an opportunity for Mr Priestly to flee the country. A Grand Jury was to be convened within four weeks from this date to evaluate the evidence. International legalities had to be reviewed since the crime was committed in another country.

Daniela had not seen the Moores since that night. Alex dropped off her to close to the train station parking lot. She walked the mile to her car in case a security camera filmed her. No cameras would not see her and Alex together. She had Grant's spare phone with a disposable sim card. The Moores would occasionally text short messages like 'Okay?' or 'G OK.'

As soon as the news broke, she called Cindy. Cindy was at her house within minutes. 'I told Tony I had to take you to the hospital. What the hell is going on?' She demanded.

'Cindy, regardless of what you hear or what is being said, don't believe it. It will be resolved. Please don't try to defend Grant. Please, please, please do not say anything about me and Grant. Nothing!!!!'

'Aren't the police or the press or someone find out about you?'

'I hope not. I don't think so.'

'I can't believe he killed her. He spent years grooming her and then....' Cindy hoped her friend could tell her something reassuring.

'Cindy, he did neither. I honestly can't say anything else. Nothing. Please! Not a word. I am not kidding or exaggerating. Literally – lives are depending on your silence.'

Cindy did not feel better; however, she did feel less scared for her friend.

# Chapter 25

The top news story for the following week concerned Grant's arrest and interpretation from every aspect of the case. Daniela had to hear theories and every imaginative fantasy of the homicide with an expressionless appearance. Quite a few people stated they knew the true story. One morning, Brian was bragging to people in the office that he had Grant Priestly's true worth from the start. He and Ken knew there was something fishy immediately after meeting him. Ken nodded like a bobblehead toy. Caroline shed a few tears over the situation. She could only say, 'But he was so nice.' Only Daniela did not put forth an opinion. When pressed what she thought about the situation, she would only say that there must be more to the case than they knew about.

Any organization or person that was touched by Grant was being dissected. Priestly Enterprises Board of Directors made several changes. Grant Priestly was placed on immediate leave of absence, with all assets frozen until further investigation. Adrian King was also immediately suspended from the firm due to being one of Mr Priestly's attorneys. Julia Wycombe became Priestly's acting CEO.

While Caroline was on holiday, Daniela was instructed to attend the HMA meeting. Karen Henderson was named Chairperson of the organization. Any pretension of following a normal agenda was quickly dispelled. Daniela listened to the various comments that ran around the conference table. It was so hard for her to remain tight-lipped when she wanted to scream, 'You don't know what you are talking about!'

Daniela never felt so alone in her life. The briefest of texts from the Moores did little to give her any peace of mind. Lack of knowledge led to sleepless nights. She could barely motivate herself to continue with any aspect of her life. She wanted to contact the Slyvia to see if they had additional details, but she knew she couldn't.

Information regarding Rachel's murder was brutal. The girl had been on a school-sanctioned field trip to Prague in the Czech Republic. The expedition includes visits to Prague Castle and the Prague Orlo or the Prague medieval astronomical clock. Of course, legends regarding the clock were expounded at length when it was being retold. A creative journalist linked the six-hundred-year-old curse with the tragic murder of a teenage American girl.

The only concrete facts known were that there were twenty female students and three chaperons staying at the Cloister Inn. Rachel Priestly and her roommate, Mia Thyes, must have crept out of their bedroom windows since there were no videotapes of them in any of the communal areas or exiting from any of the four outside doors. When neither showed up for breakfast the following morning, the chaperone immediately contacted the hotel security. A security camera filmed two fuzzy figures sneaking out of the lens' frame. Armed with this information, the police began searching the wooded area around the Inn. Within hours, the body of a teenage girl was found in a small clearing only yards away from the Inn. The barely recognizable mutilated body was transported to the local morgue.

Clothes, personal information in the purse, and a general description of the body identified the victim as Miss Rachel Tanya Priestly. Ian Priestly traveled with his sister-in-law to Prague. Sobbing in front of the vast international camera crew, she admitted that she could not bear to see her beautiful daughter in this condition. Ian confirmed that the body was indeed his niece. Where was Rachel's roommate?

Where was Mia Thyes? Immediate search parties were organized. The consensus was that another body would be found.

Mia's parents were in the Arnhem Land Australian outback researching Aboriginal kinship culture when they were finally informed about the circumstances occurring on their daughter's field trip. The Thyes arrived in Prague three days after the homicide, unaware that their daughter was still missing. Where was Mia? they demanded.

There was no answer. The Police of the Czech Republic began a nationwide search on every means of transportation once they realized that Miss Thyes was not with her fellow students. Mia's pictures flashed on all media sites. The unanswered questions naturally led to Grant Priestly, what had he done with Mia? What led the police to question suspect Mr. Priestly? A DNA report was expedited of the various materials at the crime scene. One of the DNA results illustrated a relationship match to Miss Priestly. When Mrs. Priestly volunteered to the police, the only people who were aware of Rachel's field trip were herself and, as she sobbed into her heirloom white deep lace handkerchief, her stepson Grant must have also have learned of her trip.

Two days after returning from the Czech Republic, Tiffany demanded that her daughter's body be dispatched to Rochester. Less than twenty-four hours later, it was leaked to a local reporter that Mrs. Tiffany Priestly had filed a three million dollar lawsuit against Maryvale for Young Ladies and the Cluster Inn for not protecting her daughter.

The Czech Republic General Crime Division stated they were unable to release Miss Priestly's remains until the homicide had been fully investigated. The location of Miss Thyes was a frightening mystery. How could a fifteen-year-old Swiss schoolgirl disappear? Fervent prayers were made that another body would not be found.

Various police force representations questioned Grant not only once a day but multiple times. Grant remained strangely calm during the process. Even when he was shown pictures of the mutilated body, his reaction was unexpectedly detached. The remoteness was baffling. People who were being interviewed were specifically questioned for their opinions regarding the relationship between Miss Priestly and her older brother. The responses was primarily positive. When the subject arose about the Priestly arrest, depending upon who was speaking, either Priestly was guilty like all psychopaths, or he was 100% innocent.

Priestly Enterprises was in a state of inertia. Whether it was the executive board members or employees in the mailroom staff, they could not avoid speculating about the situation. Management teams attempted to keep all projects moving and active. Marketing and Sales Department staff found that as soon as the word Priestly was mentioned, they could go no further.

The Thyes were frantic. Where was their daughter? After twenty-four hours in Prague, Mrs Thyes could no longer remain there. Her husband remained; however, she needed to return to their home. Maybe… just maybe… Mia could she find her way home.

# Chapter 26

Daniela was grateful that she decided to take only one class and it was only two weeks into the semester. Since she could barely keep her mind on her tasks at Rowe, she knew she had absolutely no chance of managing two classes. As the teacher lectured during the one class she had attended, not one word he was saying made sense to her. Daniela seriously considered withdrawing from the class as if it was a waste of time and tuition fees.

The only person she could have a conversation with was Cindy since Grant's arrest. She did not want to connect with anyone else. Daniela appeared at her job during the day and the Friday rotation at Roselyn House, but there were no other appointments on her calendar. When she was asked to go out with friends, she made excuses that she had family activities. Little Richie had his third birthday the previous Saturday. She had to attend. She made a getaway with the excuse that she was sure she was coming down with a head cold. With three households that included babies and toddlers, it was enough to get Daniela out of there quickly.

The Indian summer was making its appearance on Friday afternoon, which seemed to give a lie to the frustration Daniela was feeling. As people were leaving work for the weekend, it looked like the advertisers were making their money. It was not unusual for windshields to be papered with flyers from local restaurants. Today, the flyers were advertising the weekend football party-size pizza specials. As Daniela pulled the flyer out from under the windshield wipers, she noticed a handwritten note on her flyer. Giving a glance around the parking lot, she placed the note on the seat next to her and drove home. Resisting the urge to read the note until she reached her townhouse, she stuffed it in her bag. As soon as she closed her front door, she pulled it out. Scribble on it were the words - *Starbucks Brooke 7.*

Daniela attempted to recognize the writing, but she couldn't. Glancing at the clock, it was 6:15. Changing into jeans, she decided to do what the note ordered her to do. As she pulled into Starbucks on Brooke Avenue, it was 6:45 pm. She ordered a latte, sat in a booth, opened a book, and pretended to read while sipping the drink. It was nearly 7:15 when a couple walked past her booth as they headed toward the door. The man, who was closest to her, stopped and picked up a phone lying on the floor. 'Excuse me, Ma'am, is this your phone?'

Daniela looked at the phone in his extended hand. Glancing at the couple, the attractive blonde beside him winked. Daniela took the phone and said hesitantly. 'Oh! Thank You. I didn't even realize it fell out of my purse.' As she took the phone, they left without another word. She forced herself to stay in the booth for another fifteen minutes while she finished her drink. Then calmly… calmly… calmly… she left the coffee shop.

Daniela did not want to go home. Driving to the Canandaigua pier, she parked. Pulling out the phone, she realized that it wasn't a cell phone. It was a recorder. 'All right,' she thought, 'this is becoming shades of Mission Impossible.' For the first time in weeks, she smiled. Turning the recorder on play, a familiar voice spoke. Sylvia said quietly. 'Tomorrow at 10 am go to Eastview Mall Shopping Center. Park near the food court entrance. As close to 10:30 am as possible, leave the Mall through the Dick's Sporting Goods entrance. Walking out, you will see a White Chevy Cargo Van parked near the entrance. Open the door in the second section and get in. You will be joined in about 5 minutes.' Daniela expected the recorder to go up in smoke at the end of the message. She sat for a moment to process what just happened over the last ninety minutes. Hopefully, Alex? Or Sylvia had some news for her. Please let it be Grant who joined her in the van. She did not cry over Rachel because she knew she wasn't dead. She was just as sure that Grant did not kill anyone. But what was going on? It had been nine days since Grant's arrest. Every day, she was hearing more alleged stories. Some of them were becoming extremely outlandish. The recent hypothesis was that Grant was the head, or at least an interested participant, of a local sex slave ring. Every teenage disappearance for the last twenty years was being compared to Grant's timeline. Taking several deep breaths to calm down, Daniela listened to the message two more times before she put her plans into action.

Placing the recorder in her purse, she pulled out her phone and called Cindy. Before she said a word, her friend's voice asked. 'Dani, what is happening?'

'What are your plans for tonight?'

'Not much. We just had pizza delivered. Do you want to come over?'

'Nope. But I want you to come over to my house.' Danelle spoke with a measured, calm voice.

'I'm not going to ask any questions now. Would an hour be okay? I want to get the kids settled down for the night.

'Have you told Tony about… anything?'

'Not a word. I promise.

'You're a good friend.'

When Daniela went home, she could not imagine what would be happening the next day, but she tried to be as prepared as she could be. Carrying a tote or even a larger-than-normal handbag could be a red flag to someone somewhere if they got a trace that she was involved with Grant. Or so she imagined. She picked out an outfit for the following day. Hoping the morning would be cool, she pulled out a non-descriptive fleece. In the pockets, she stuffed a couple of pairs of clean underwear. Matching underwear, of course, because you know the cliché that you never can tell when you will be rushed to the hospital. Or, in her case, maybe kidnapped would be a better substitute. Kidnapped wearing her granny panties? Not in her lifetime. Zipping her passport and phone charger into a side pocket of her purse, she felt a little more prepared. An hour later, Cindy was on her doorstep. For the neighbor's sake, she greeted Cindy as if this was a surprise visit.

After ushering Cindy into the house, she said, 'Dani, are you going for an Oscar or something?'

'No. I am just so glad to see you.' Daniela turned the volume up on the television. Sitting down on the sofa, she pulled out the recorder and played it for Cindy.

After listening to the recording for the third time, Cindy exclaimed, 'Are you freaking kidding!!! You are not going to do what it says! Dani, I have gone along with lots of screwy things that you wanted to do, but I can't go along with what you are planning!'

Daniela was taken aback by her friend's reaction. 'That is Sylvia. They obviously have something to tell me. It must be important.'

'They work for a man who is imprisoned for murder!!!'

Realizing that Cindy was really upset, Daniela tried to find the words to calm her down. 'What can I do to make you understand that I'm not in any danger?'

'Go to the police. Tell them everything. Don't you think they can solve this far better than you? A girl is dead. I don't want you to be the next one!'

Daniela knew her instincts were right. Grant has nothing to do with any death. Using a humbler tone, she tried again, 'Cindy, I need your help.'

'Go to the police. Help done!'

'Can we do a comprise?' Cindy glared at her. 'What if both of us go to Eastview Mall?' As Cindy was about to interrupt, Daniela held up her hand. 'You can park by where the Chevy van is parked. Meet me at the food court. We can walk out together through Dicks Sporting Goods, and you can take tons of pictures of the van in case I go missing.'

'That is the stupidest plan I ever heard. I am not going to help you get kidnapped. Why did you ask me to come over?'

'Because I wanted you to Cat home with you for a few days. I am sure I am going to be gone for that long.'

'What are you going to do with your car? It will get fined or impounded or both.'

Looking guilty at her friend, Daniela admitted she hadn't thought that far ahead. Cindy sighed. 'Dani, I can't believe I was excited when you first told me about Grant. Now I wish you never met up with him. Okay, I have a suggestion. We will comprise on your comprise. What if you park at the food court entrance like the instructions say? I will park where the Chevy van is parked. The kids and Tony will come with me. We will meet up in the food court. You can walk with Tony and the kids to the van through the Dick's Sporting Goods Store entrance. He and the kids get into the car. Meanwhile, I will leave the food court and take your car home.'

'What will Tony say about me disappearing in the van?'

Chuckling, Cindy said, 'That will be the easiest part. You are going away with a married man for the weekend.'

Laughing with her friend, Daniela, remarked without heat, 'You bitch.' Leaning over, she hugged her.

'I'm still not happy over the situation. But I am going to get the license plate number and as many pictures as possible. I promise you if we find your body parts in different parts of the country, I am only buying one funeral wreath.'

'Will you take Cat?'

'Now you are pushing our friendship.' Twenty minutes later, Cindy left not only with Cat but with the extra key to Daniela's car.

# Chapter 27

The next morning at 9:30 am, Daniela took a deep breath as she locked her front door. She responded to the greeting from Mandy and her husband as they were also getting into their car. Ten minutes later, she entered the food court entrance. It wasn't long until she saw Cindy, Tony, Sarah, and Allen. After they greeted Auntie Dani – Auntie by affection, not blood– they returned to their demands for promised purchases from their mother and stepfather. When Cindy requested Tony to take the children to Dicks' to start looking for new sneakers, he didn't utter one word of complaint. Being a wonderful husband, he kissed his wife gently on the lips as he whispered, 'I hope I don't have to bail you out of jail.' Meanwhile, Daniela had already exited the scene to the nearby mall restrooms.

Cindy entered one of the stalls. Looking under the divider between the toilets she saw a blue fleece, similar to her yellow one being thrust towards her. Passing the blue fleece toward her friend, Daniela also pushed her purse to Cindy. Entering the contents of her purse into Daniela's handbag, she flushed the toilet and opened the door. Two other women were washing their hands at the sink. Daniela emerged from her stall. As they washed their hands, they stared at each other in the mirror. Daniela gave her friend a quick wink and left the women's restroom.

Within minutes, Daniela located Tony and the children as they finished paying for their sneakers. Sarah squeak, 'Auntie Dani, you're wearing mommy's coat!'

Daniela leaned toward the children. 'Mommy is going to play a trick on Tony. She is going to sneak home before we get there. Do you think she can do it?'

The six and four-year-old children's eyes widened at the thought of fooling their stepfather. Solemnly, they both nodded their heads. Straightening up, she said to the children while looking at Tony. 'Let's see who can get home first.'

Just as they were ready to exit the mall's double doors, Dani asked. 'What kind of sneakers did you get?' Both children began to crowd around her, excited to talk about the colors, designs, and whose sneakers were the best sneakers in the whole wide world. Tony's Ford Explorer was parked in the space directly beside the Chevy Van. Bless Tony! He parked his car so the passenger door was facing the van's passenger door. When he opened the passenger side for the children and 'wife', Daniela was able to slide open the passenger side of the van at the same time. The children were belted into their car seats before they realized that Auntie Dani was not in the car with them. As they began to voice their questions, Tony pulled out of the parking lot.

The van's second row of seats was split seat design. Behind the driver's seat and on the passenger's side, the divided seats which could be folded flat. The seat next to Daniela was already in the flattened position. There are no windows on the van's sides, the driver and passenger's windows were tinted. Daniela attempted to blend in with the seat. It seemed as if an eternity had passed, or was it closer to five minutes? The side door slid open. Alex's body protected anyone from looking inside. His arms were filled with cardboard storage boxes from Pennys' Department Store. He spoke very softly as he began arranging the boxes. 'The house is being watched since Mr Priestly's arrest. I hate to ask you, but I need you to get on the floor. These boxes are light. I am going to put them on top of you. Sometimes, they check when we go in and out.' Before he finished speaking, Daniela did what he had asked.

Without a doubt, being on the floor of a cargo van with cardboard boxes covering her was not the smoothest ride she had ever had. Her whole body tensed when she heard Alex whisper, 'Being stopped.' The next sound was the automatic window being rolled down. 'Good morning, Officer.'

'Good morning, Mr. Moore. You look like you have been busy this morning.'

'Definitely have been. For the last month, some of the churches held donation drives for the Roselyn and Gardner's Homeless Shelters. I find that bringing boxes to transport the donations makes it easier on collection day.'

For a few seconds, the officer said nothing. 'That is a very worthy cause. By the way, I know it has been a few days, but have you remembered anything strange that happened around those days that Mr. Priestly was away?'

With reluctance in his voice, Alex responded, 'No, I told the other officers everything I know.'

Hitting the roof of the van with the palm of his hand, the office concluded, 'Well, if you do, I hope you will let us know. Good luck with the donation drive.'

Alex pressed the garage door opener as he continued up the driveway. 'Miss Weiss, stay down there just for another minute.' As Daniela heard the garage door hit the cement floor, the passenger door opened. Alex began to pull the boxes off. The door connecting the kitchen and garage opened.

# Chapter 28

Daniela barely made it into the kitchen when Sylvia announced, 'Miss Rachel is safe.'

The weight which has been holding her down, suddenly dropped from her shoulder. 'When did you find out?'

'Three days ago.'

'THREE DAYS AGO!!!' She stared in disbelief at the Moores. 'I have been worried sick and….'

'Miss Wiess, please sit down.' Sylvia and Alex also seated themselves at the table. Alex placed a cup of coffee in front of her. Sylvia patted her hand. 'We couldn't tell you until today.'

There were an unending number of questions she wanted to ask. Where to begin? 'Then whose body was found? Mia Thyes?

'Unfortunately, it was Mia.'

The coffee remained untouched as she sank her face into her hands. 'The poor Thyes.' Raising her face, 'Where is Rachel?'

Pushing the coffee cup toward her, Alex answered, 'This is where we need you.'

'And what is happening about Grant?'

'You must trust us. This is his plan.'

Daniela needed a moment to process the new information. Raising the coffee mug to her lips, she looked at the Moores. Gently asking, 'Does any of this have to do with the Grant's blackmailing?'

Alex responded, 'Miss Wiess..'

'Daniela.'

'Daniela,' Alex started over. 'Neither I nor Sylvia know everything that has transpired but we know he was framed. Mr King has been staying away from us and anyone connected to Mr Priestly. We are all being watched. That includes Laura.'

'His assistant? Was she the one who dropped the recorder?'

'Actually, it was her fiancé, but yes.'

'How does Rachel and her poor friend fit into this? I am really confused.'

'Daniela, you're the only one police have not been watching because there is no connection between you and Mr Priestly.'

'Of course, I will do anything I can do to help. I am sure you know that!'

Sylvia asked, 'Does anyone know where you are?'

'My friend, Cindy. She helped me today. She only knows about the message to meet at the mall.'

'Was that her husband and children parked next to the van?'

Daniela was feeling guilty about getting Cindy involved. Defensibly, she replied. 'Yes, but her husband doesn't know anything about the message. He thinks I am going away for the weekend with a married man.'

For the first time, the Moores smiled at her. Daniela relaxed slightly. Alex asked, 'Are you sure your friend won't tell her husband or anyone else?'

'A million times positive.'

Sylvia took over the conversation. 'Daniela, do you have a passport? Even if you don't have it on you.' Sticking her hand in Cindy's purse, Daniela laid the passport on the table. 'Excellent. We can't tell you everything because we don't know everything.'

# Chapter 29

Adrain King spent nearly every day at Attica Correctional Facility with Grant Priestly. The hour-long distance between Rochester and Attica was worlds away from each other. Whether it was written or verbal, Adrian and Grant were extremely cautious about their conversations. Since Grant returned from Europe, small puzzle pieces began to fall into place. It didn't take long for both men to become aware of how dangerous Grant's situation had become. More importantly, there were a few larger pieces of evidence that were not yet uncovered. The homicide case against Grant had an additional problematic fact.

Since the murder was committed in one country and the primary suspect was in another, the Czech Republic government was within its rights to request Mr. Grant Priestly to be extradited and tried in the Czech Republic according to Article 3(2) of the Agreement on Mutual Legal Assistance between the United States of America and the European Union signed in Washington on 25 June 2003. Adrian was quite aware of the Agreement. However, he was using every manoeuver in his attorney's arsenal to prevent the extradition from taking place. In addition to the local police investigators, Mr Priestly was also being questioned by Interpol and the FBI.

News agencies from around the world who were staking out Oakfield Street and Priestly Enterprise now included the Attica Correctional Facility. Grant Priestly's Attorney refused to give statements to the press. This lack of information left people like Mr Priestly's brother, Ian, and his father's second wife, Tiffany Priestly, to give details and updates on the investigation. Tiffany Priestly did not neglect to mention the continued saga of having Miss Priestly's remains still in Prague.

The news media continued to contact anyone, or any organization, who was even slightly acquainted with the primary suspect. Various social service agencies began to investigate charities or organizations to verify if Mr Priestly had performed any improper activities while he was part of their group.

Grant attempted to refrain from thinking about any aspect of his life that he was unable to manage at this time. He knew he was innocent and everything will be resolved. He could only hope that Priestly executives would manage the business in the most suitable manner possible under these agonizing conditions. Late at night, when he couldn't do anything but think, he allowed thoughts of Daniela to become forefront in his mind. To keep everyone safe, Grant made sure that his siblings, the Moores, Laura, or anyone else who would be interested in visiting didn't come near him. He received hand-drawn cards from his nieces and nephews. He appreciated the words of encouragement and love from his sisters that were included in each card.

Even though his mail and other correspondence were scrutinized by the authorities, he also received several repulsive letters or drawings about what should happen to men who murdered young girls.

When the news reporters questioned officers from Interpol and the FBI, they were as tight-lipped as the suspect and his attorney.

The only benefit Grant received from the NY State Correctional Facilities was a solitary cell. The cell was allowed due to multiple threats against his life. After the prison lights went out, Grant would lie awake thinking about what was happening and how could he protect those he loved from while he was in a jail cell. He spent night after night putting different parts together until the only possible solution remained. Nearly two weeks had passed after his arrest. Adrian agreed with Grant that the last puzzle piece had been found, and it fitted flawlessly in the whole scenario.

Neither Grant nor Adrian considered for a moment to inform the local police force. Interpol was only concerned with one aspect of the homicide. The Czech police representative who came to the prison seemed highly suspicious when Adrian suggested that they should consider investigating another theory.

It was at this time Grant brought Daniela's name up for the first time. Adrian was amazed and speechless when Grant explained that they had been dating for nearly seven months. 'Who knew about her?'

'Sylvia and Alex. Laura knows there is someone in my life but has not met her. More importantly, Rachel knows Daniela.'

'Could Rachel have told some like her mother?'

With a snort of derision, Grant answered, 'I highly doubt it.'

'How about this girl? Has she told anyone about you?'

'The girl's name is Daniela Weiss.' Grant responded coldly.

'I was not insulting her, but you have to admit, there are a lot of moving parts in your case.'

'Adrian, I would trust her with my life.'

Gathering his papers together, Adrian remarked drily, 'I think you just have. Hopefully, next week, this nightmare will be over.'

# Chapter 30

Grant has no idea how Adrian arranged it, but thirty-six hours after he told Adrian about Daniela, the date had been included on the court calendar before the Honorable Judge Richard Wilkinson. How Adrian managed to get a date set on the court calendar within such a short time was amazing.

The official explanation for the session was that the suspect was expected to change his not-guilty plea to what? No one knew. Mr Priestly's options were limited. He could plead not guilty, guilty, or no contest.

Since court proceedings were a matter of public record, it was not surprising that every seat in the courtroom was filled and people were spilling into the hallway. In the row behind Mr Grant Priestly were the defendants' sisters, Mrs Eleanor Robertson and Mrs Mariah Gordon. Mr. King had requested their presence but did not explain why.

In the seats behind the prosecuting attorney were the victim's mother, Mrs. Tiffany Priestly, and the defendant's brother, Mr. Ian Priestly.

When Judge Wilkinson entered the courtroom, he had to use the gravel several times for silence. Surveying the crowded room, he began.

'This is a special session which I agreed to hold in light of some additional evidence.'

The prosecuting attorney immediately stood up. 'Why was I not informed of this additional evidence?'

'Mr. Galan, it is to my understanding that the evidence only arrived at one am this morning.'

Barely keeping the disdain from his voice, he responded to the judge. 'It is to be appreciated that Mr King was able to schedule a date on your calendar so quickly.'

Snickers were heard throughout the room; Judge Wilkinson applied his gravel again. 'Mr. Galan, I am not responsible to you for what my court does and does not do. If you have any other similar comments, I recommend you keep them to yourself.' The Judge looked around the room before he made his next remarks. 'I want everyone to notice that we have additional personnel in the courtroom. We have officers from Interpol who are attending this session for a specific purpose.' Due to the conversational buzz surmising about the reasons, Judge Wilkinson again used the gavel several times before silence descended.

'Mr Grant Priestly, would you please rise?' Both Adrian and Grant stood up. 'Mr Priestly, do you wish to change your plea?'

'No, Your Honor, I do not.' The noise raised to a roar. Why was this session called if he wasn't going to change his plea? The gavel was applied again to force the courtroom into silence.

'Mr. King, what is the meaning of this?' Judge Wilkinson demanded.

'Your Honor, Mr Priestly is innocent, and we would like to have all charges dismissed.' Adrain turned to the courtroom door and slightly nodded his head. The door opened to admit a sturdy black woman beside a scared blonde teenager.

A scream rose from Tiffany Priestly. 'RACHEL… ' Ian leaped to his feet at the same time and exclaimed, 'What the fuck!' If the courtroom noise was loud previously, for the next few minutes, the scene was deafening. Tiffany tried to reach her daughter. The bailiff blocked her path, and she was forced to let her daughter walk past her. Hanfeeh moved one step closer to the girl. Rachel glanced once at her mother and then looked at the Judge as she went towards the front of the room. When Rachel reached her half-sisters, she sat next to them without saying a word. Hanfeeh sat in the seat directly behind Rachel. Mariah and Eleanor couldn't keep their eyes off her.

Meanwhile, Tiffany was screaming and crying, 'My Baby, my Baby!' Then she turned on Ian. 'You told me she was dead. You knew she was alive!'

'She was dead! Just like I told you!' He screamed back at her.

At this point, the sound of the gavel did not make a dent. The Bailiff's voice overpowered their screaming match. 'The room is to come to order.'

Judge Wilkinson said very sternly. 'Mrs. Priestly. Mr Priestly. Sit down. If there is another word from either of you, both of you will be removed from this room under detention.' Changing his tone, he addressed Rachel gently. 'Miss Priestly, can you come up here to the bench?' She looked petrified. The room was so silent. No one wanted to miss a word.

Hanfeeh stood up. 'Your Honor, may I also join Miss Priestly? I will not speak unless requested.'

'May I ask who you are and your role in this case?'

'My name is Hanfeeh Keneayo. I am a social worker for Monroe County.'

'Have you known Miss Priestly for long?'

'No, Your Honor. I met Miss Priestly for the first-time last night when she was brought to the Roselyn House.'

Looking back at the teenager, the Judge as kindly, 'Miss Priestly, would you feel better if Mrs. Keneayo came to the front of the room with you.'

Rachel nodded her head. With the crowded room staring at the event in front of them, very few people noticed another person walking from the back of the room to the defendant's side of the room. Sylvia and Alex moved closer so that Daniela could sit beside them. Grant turned his head slightly and nodded. Her 100-watt smile appeared.

As Rachel was being sworn in, Tiffany was weeping loudly. After the first glance at her mother when she entered the courtroom, Rachel did not even look at her again. At the Judge's request, Hanfeeh stood just a little behind the witness chair. She was close enough to bring reassurance to the girl but not close enough to influence any responses. Before the Judge began speaking to Rachel, he made one warning to Tiffany. 'Mrs Priestly, if you are unable to control yourself, I request you to leave the courtroom.' Then, he addressed the two attorneys. 'Due to unique circumstances, I will be questioning Miss Priestly for the time being.

Ensuring that Tiffany was following his instruction, Judge Wilkinson leaned over his bench to talk directly to the scared young girl. 'Miss Priestly, please face me and try to ignore the other people here. I am going to ask you some questions. Just tell me the answers. Do you understand?' Rachel nodded. The Judge asked Rachel the first question. 'Is your name Rachel Priestly?' Rachael nodded her head. 'Miss Priestly, you need to verbally your answers my questions. The court stenographer,' pointing to the person in front of the judge's bench, 'needs to record your answers.'

Taking a deep breath, Rachel responded, 'Yes, I am Rachel Priestly.'

'Miss Priestly, if you have difficulty answering these next questions, please let me know, all right?'

Once again, she nodded her head until she remembered the Judge's instructions. 'Yes, Sir.

The Judge turned to address the courtroom, he remarked uncompromisingly. 'If there is one sound from anyone in this room, I will have the courtroom immediately cleared. Do you understand!' He waited until he saw nods from most of the assemblage.

Turning back to the frightened teenager, he asked. 'Miss Priestly, how old are you?

'Fifteen,' She responded in a quivering voice.

'You are one of the bravest people I have ever met. Take your time in answering my next question. Did you know that many people thought you were,' trying to choose his words carefully, 'that you were no longer alive?'

'Yes.'

'Did you know that your brother was arrested?'

'Not until later.'

'Miss Priestly,' Judge Wilkinson said gently. 'Can you tell me what happened?'

Rachel's eyes filled up with tears as she put her hands over her face and began to sob, 'I can't. I can't.' Hanfeeh placed her hand on Rachel's shoulder.

There was a collected silence in the room as frightening girl's sobs filled the atmosphere. Adrain King rose. 'Your Honor, may I and the prosecuting attorney approach the bench?' The Judge motioned them forward as he turned off his microphone. For the longest three minutes, only hush whispers and sobbing were heard.

The Judge then motioned both attorneys back. Turning on the microphone. Judge Wilkinson spoke, 'Bailiff, please escort Miss Priestly and Mrs. Keneayo to my chambers.' As Rachel stood up from the witness chair, Tiffany also stood and began to complain, 'I want to go with my daughter. She is my daughter. Why are they separating us?' The Judge's gavel cut through her arguments. The bailiff closed the door behind him.

'Mrs. Priestly, remain seated! It has been brought to my attention that Miss Priestly was escorted to Rochester by an Interpol Officer.' The shocked silence was followed by a growing buzz.

Without any warning, Tiffany Priestly jumped up again. Her martyr mother's demeanor was gone. Facing Ian Priestly, she screamed, 'You told me she was dead! You can't do anything right.' Judge Wilkinson did not move as the dramatic scene began to unfold.

Ian's temper, never the calmest under any circumstances, totally exploded as he began to yell back at his stepmother. 'Shut up, You Stupid Bitch. They have nothing on us.'

Judge Wilkinson decided that now it was time to interrupt. Applying his gavel again, 'Will the officers of the court please remove Mrs. Tiffany Priestly and Mr. Ian Priestly?' Tiffany was refusing the let the officer touch her. Ian threatened Grant as he left the room.

No one else was leaving the courtroom. The news media personnel were typing on their devices as fast as their fingers could move.

Judge Wilkinson spoke in a calm and measured voice. 'The motion before the court today was a request from the defensive attorney to withdraw the charges of first-degree murder against Mr. Grant Priestly. We are not hearing any other information about other aspects regarding this case.' The Judge waited for a few seconds while the spectators exchanged their comments. When the courtroom was quiet again, he continued. 'Mr. Svoboda is an official representative from Interpol. Both Miss Priestly and Mr. Svoboda arrived early this morning. Mr. King, would you like to call your witness?'

Mr. Svoboda's stocky body was nearly 6-foot-tall. He created an image of a person very few people would like to anger. His thick, curly, dark black hair with grey streaks gave him an air of authority. Whether it was because he had been traveling all night or if it was natural, his face's 5 o'clock shadow was evident even though it was not yet noon. Despite the fact he was heavy-set, he strode self-assuredly to the witness stand.

Sitting in the witness box, he was asked by the Bailiff, 'Mr. Svoboda, do you wish to take your oath on the Bible?'

With a strong Czech accent, he responded, 'I am Officer Svoboda. I do not have any religion.'

Judge Wilkinson interrupted, 'Officer Svoboda, I apologize for the court for not addressing you by your proper title.'

The Bailiff continued, 'Please raise your right hand. Do you solemnly, sincerely, and truly declare and affirm that the evidence you shall give shall be the truth, the whole truth, and nothing but the truth? '

Officer Svoboda responded solemnly, 'I do.'

Adrain King arose and walked to the witness stand. 'Officer Svoboda, were you one of Miss Priestly's escorts?'

'I was.'

'What was your role within the Interpol concerning Miss Thyes's death and Miss Priestly's disappearance?'

'Due to the international circumstances of the case, I was assigned to work with the Czech police and, later, the American FBI.'

'Officer Svoboda, how do you know that Mr. Grant Priestly was not involved with Miss Thyes' death and Miss Priestly's disappearance?'

For the next twenty minutes, Officer Svoboda laid out the procedure of what had been happening since the discovery of the homicide. There were times when he began to explain certain aspects. At those times, Judge Wilkinson's gavel would interrupt with the comment, 'That does not pertain to this case.'

While the explanation was continuing, Eleanor and Mariah were holding each other hands as tears slid down their cheeks. They were not as close to their half-sister as Grant, but as mothers, they could not imagine either of the daughters experiencing what Rachel went through.

At the end of Officer Svoboda's testimony, everyone waited. Judge Wilkinson met the eyes of the Prosecuting Attorney. Mr. Galan stood up. 'Your Honor, the State would like to withdraw the charges against Mr. Grant Priestly.'

'The charges have been withdrawn. Mr. Priestly, you are free to go.' The press corps made a mad dash to the courtroom doors to file their reports.

His sisters wrapped their arms around Grant. Adrian was shaking Grant's hand. The Prosecuting Attorney walked over and congratulated Adrian. The Judge did not leave the courtroom but once again applied the gavel.

'Bailiff, escort everyone out the courtroom except the immediate Priestly family and Mr. King.' Grant pushed through the people surrounding him to Daniela. Grabbing her hand and holding it tightly in his asked, 'Your Honor, May I ask the court's permission to have my fiancée, Miss Wiess, remain?'

Having the charges dropped against him caused less astonishment than the unexpected announcement of his fiancée. Judge Wilkinson lowered his head and peered over his eyeglass frames at Grant and Daniela. He did not remember seeing her picture at any of the recent events where Grant was present. When she first appeared in his courtroom, he assumed she was a clerk at Priestly Enterprises. Slowly, he nodded yes.

As Sylvia and Alex gave Grant a quick congratulations, Sylvia said softly in his ear, 'I will have rooms ready for everyone when you are done here.'

# Chapter 31

Judge Wilkinson unsnapped his judge's robe and laid it over his judge's chair as he stepped down from the bench. Adrain, Grant, Daniela, Eleanor, and Mariah were the only ones left in the courtroom. They took seats in front of the courtroom. Perched on the edge of the defendant's table, the Judge began, 'Miss Priestly has undergone some horrific experiences. I am deeply concerned about not only her future but her current mental well-being. She will not be returning to her mother. I would dislike her to stay under the care of Social Services until…' His voice trailed off.

Without hesitation, Grant spoke up, 'I am requesting to take temporary custody of Rachel until it can be made permanent.'

'Is the wise, Mr Priestly? I was thinking that Mrs Robertson or Mrs Gordon could include Miss Priestly in their household.

'Your Honor, this is the place that Rachel is familiar with.'

'Mr. Priestly,' interrupted Judge Wilkinson. 'Yours is a bachelor household.'

Shedding the formality to the man Grant had known for most of his adult life, 'Richard, how soon can you marry Daniela and me?'

'How long has Miss Wiess been in your life?'

'Your Honor,' Daniela was not surprised at Grant's lie about their engagement. She knew she loved him and was sure he felt the same. However, right now, Rachel was the priority in their lives. 'Grant proposed nearly a month ago. I am not wearing my engagement ring because it is getting sized. We were going to tell our families but….' She paused. 'All this happened.'

'Richard, if our marriage means the difference between having Rachel living with us or going to an unfamiliar environment…. Well, Dani, what do you think?

'Whether we get married tomorrow or next year, we are getting married. But right now, Rachel needs secure and a loving home.'

The Judge glanced at Eleanor and Miraha. 'Do either of you have an opinion?'

Eleanor started first. 'Rachel was only three years old when I married my husband. We moved to Virginia shortly after that.'

Miriah added, 'I was in college and rarely in Rochester. I don't think either Eleanor or I would mind having Rachel live with us, but Grant has been closer to her, and I think would be a better guardian.'

'Mrs Priestly's family?'

Eleanor responded. 'Tiffany was an only child. The Roberts, Tiffany's parents, live near Los Angeles.'

Richard Wilkinson didn't say a word but nodded his head. After a few seconds, he said to Grant, 'You better go to the registrar's office today and apply for your marriage license.' As he stood up, he said to the group. 'We are going into my chambers now. I feel that Miss Priestly should be admitted to Unity Hospital for the night. If nothing else, she needs a good night's sleep. Her evaluation will be for physical and emotional well-being. Mrs Kanayo has agreed to spend the night with her. None of you will be allowed to see her until tomorrow. Do you understand?' Agreements were made. 'I can't order you, but I would suggest counseling as soon as possible.'

The Judge opened the door to his chambers. When Rachel saw Grant, she left her hamburger and fries and ran to him. As she wrapped her arms around his waist, her tears began to flow. Grant's arms tightened around the trembling figure. In disjoint words, she said, 'scared… you…awful…couldn't.'

'Hey, Sweetheart. I'm here now. So is Mariah and Eleanor.' Cautiously, he added, 'So is Dani.'

Wiping her eyes and blowing her nose with the tissue Hanfeeh handed her, she said husky voice, 'Oh Gee, of course, Dani is here. She flew back with me.' Laughing, Grant hugged his sister and released her. Mariah was the first to give Rachel a hug, followed by Eleanor.

'Miss Priestly,' said the Judge formally. 'I have been talking to your family…'

'My MOTHER?' She exclaimed angrily.

'No,' said the Judge slowly. 'She will not be available for a while.'

Angrily, Rachel said, 'She wanted to kill me!'

Judge Wilkinson said, 'We don't know that for sure, Miss Priestly.' Rachel glared at the Judge. He cleared his throat uncomfortably. 'Miss Priestly, can you sit here for a moment?' He pointed to a chair in front of his desk. Everyone else seated themselves on the chambers' sofa or armchairs. 'Miss Priestly… Rachel, we are trying to do our best to help you. Tonight, you will be going to Unity Hospital so that the doctors can give you the once over.'

By myself?'

'No, Mrs. Keneayo will be spending the night with you.'

'But I don't want to go to the hospital.'

'I understand. If the doctors give you the okay, you can leave tomorrow morning.'

'Where will I go then?'

'Rachel, it is not the final decision.' He paused and asked, 'Who do you want to stay with? Your brother and sisters would like you to be part of their families.' The Judge said softly, 'Don't turn to face them. Look at me.'

Without hesitation, she responded, 'Gee… I mean Grant.'

Looking at Rachel's face, Judge Wilkinson as a follow-up question. 'And with Miss Weiss?'

Incredulity, Rachel asked, 'Dani? Of course!'

The Judge sat back in his chair for a moment, then stood up. 'Alright, Miss Priestly. Say goodnight to your family. I am sure you will be seeing them tomorrow. Mr. Kennedy,' motioning to the bailiff, 'will be taking you and Mrs Keneayo to the hospital now.' Looking at the people in the room. 'I will give you five minutes before I want you out of my chambers.'

# Chapter 32

The Priestly siblings, Adrain, and Daniela appreciated the underground corridor that led from the courthouse to the parking garage. As they were leaving, Grant and Daniela took the Judge's advice and applied for their marriage license. The Priestly sisters went to the house on Oakfield Street to call their respective spouses, giving them updates on the remarkable morning. They hoped that Grant and Daniela would not return too soon; they intended to grill Sylvia and Alex for all the missing details. Laura and Oliver were also invited to the house. Adrain refused the invitation. He was looking forward to going home and seeing his family, who had been severely neglected for the last several weeks.

News of Grant's release and the arrest of two other Priestly plus Henrik Wagner was on every newscast, newspaper, and social media. Grant was extremely grateful that Alex had hired a black Mercedes with dark-tinted windows to pick up Daniela and Grant so that they could take care of several errands. The group knew that even though the underground corridor was used by a limited amount of people, as soon as they exited, there would be a massive amount of people who tried to obtain the first quote from Grant Priestly. Before they exited, Grant spoke briefly to his sisters. Then gave a bear hug with a deep feeling of appreciation to his father's friend and his attorney. The anticipated crowd was ready for them. First, Daniela, then Grant slid into the back seat of the car. When the driver asked where to first, Grant kissed Daniela's fingers as he said, 'Nulton Jewelers.'

As the car pulled into moving traffic, Grant pulled Daniela into his arms. After several kisses, he said softly, 'I was so afraid that you were going to say you didn't want to marry me.'

As she raised her head from his shoulder, she laughed, 'After what we have been through, how could I possibly say no.'

Seriously, he asked, 'I know most women want large weddings with all the trimmings. I hate pushing you into this quick ceremony.'

'Darling, you are not even close to pushing me into anything.' Cupping his face with her hands, she kissed his lips as they pulled in front of the jewelry store. Laughing as he pulled her out of the car, he said, 'I hope we find a ring that does not need to get sized.'

Returning to the house on Oakfield Street, Eleanor, Mariah, Alex, and Sylvia were still sitting at the dining room table, picking over the remains of the luncheon that Alex had supplied them. As soon as the newly engaged couple walked into the room, questions were hurled at them. Eleanor took Grant aside and told him that she and Mariah had gone to Grandmother Lucy's house. They had brought her to the house on Oakfield Street. She was sleeping upstairs.

'OMG, Eleanor, look at this ring,' Mariah raised Daniela's hand. Eleanor disengaged herself from her brother to examine Daniela's engagement ring.

'Grant, did you finally develop good taste, or did Daniela pick it out? What a beautiful opal. Can you see the deep blue greens? This must be a custom design. The bezel has such a gorgeous diamond halo. I love the asymmetric diamond split shank.'

Grant laughed as he said, 'Sweetie, this is what you will hear since Eleanor's husband is a jewelry designer.'

'Daniela, you should be grateful. This tightwad will not try to pawn off any cubic zirconia on you while I am around.'

Over coffee in the library, he began the history of the last several months. Grant also included the Moores, Laura, and Oliver since they played an active role in the events; however, no one knew the entire saga.

# Chapter 33

'Six months ago.' Grant began, 'Henrik received a blackmail threat which was sent to me. As Sylvia, Alex, Laura, and' nodding to his fiancée, 'Dani knows.' He was holding Dani's hands in his, 'I am sure they told you about the blackmail threat. However, at the time, Dani, asked me how did the blackmailer know what amount I could afford? That aspect did not dawn on me until later. When it did, I realized that it had to be someone who knew me and Priestlys' Enterprises.'

Taking a slip of his coffee, Grant continued. 'I'm not sure how much you are aware of how Dad created his will.'

Eleanor spoke it. 'Weren't all the assets to be divided equally amongst us, with Tiffany getting her widow's share?'

'Close, but not exactly. Dad had Tiffany's number shortly after their marriage. But Tiffany continuously threatened to keep Rachel away from him, and he didn't want to lose contact with Rachel nor a long drawn out legal entanglement. Another part that played into this disaster was Ian.'

'I can't believe that Ian set you up like this!' exclaimed Mariah.

Shaking his head, ' I couldn't believe it either – at the time. Ian not only spent all the cash he could get his hands on, but he was stealing money from Grandma.' Daniela nodded as the rest of the people exclaimed in anger. 'As far as Tiffany's share of Dad's estate goes, he left the minimum he could. All the siblings have a shared part of the business; that we knew. But Dad left, in addition to Rachel's corporate shares there were several other assets that he had bequeaths to her. Dad changed the will just before his death. That is when I found out about Rachel's additional assets. They include their house. Tiffany can live there until Rachel decides to sell it. There were a couple of other assets that I am sure Tiffany expected to be given to her.'

Grant waited until some of the information was absorbed. 'If Rachel died underage, naturally, everything would be passed to Tiffany.'

Laura asked the question they had all been thinking, 'Why didn't Tiffany know about Rachel's inheritance? Also, how and why did Henrik get involved?'

'Tiffany and Henrik have been having an affair since before Dad's death. Adrain only found out recently and he told me.' Once again, there were exclamations such as 'Bitch! What! OMG!'

Grant said, 'Tiffany did know about some of Rachel's inheritance. Her remarks at the time were that it didn't make any difference. As far as Henrik was concerned, believe me, it took us a while to put this all together. The private detective Henrik told me he had hired is currently a Rochester police detective. Definitely crooked. That is why neither I nor Adrian dared say anything about what was happening. We didn't know who was doing what. Unfortunately, Rachel was involved by accident, even though I am sure she would have been a victim of an accident before her eighteenth birthday. Rachel knew I was being extorted.' Nodding to the Moores, 'I'm sure that Sylvia and Alex told you that part. When Rachel tried to tell me that I was in danger, she had received a text from Tiffany's phone. It said - *The time is now.* It was sent by accident.' Grant paused for another slip of the cold coffee.

'When Tiffany told Ian about the misdirected text, they decided to push their plans forward.' Of course, Tiffany had the details of the school trip. Fortunately, Rachel also has sent me a copy. While I was in the air heading to Prague, I managed to get a hold of Adrian. He contacted Fritz Munitz, with whom we had worked together a few times. By the time I landed, Mia was dead.'

'What happened?' Eleanor asked quietly.

'I don't know if you ever saw Mia. She and Rachel could be sisters. They look so much alike. Don't ask me to explain it, but they decided to swap their clothes and IDs. Mia wanted to pretend she was an American and Rachel wanted to be a Swiss when decided to sneak for some fun in the Prague. It seems that they met some locals earlier. For whatever reason, they were swapping their clothes in the woods near the hotel instead of their rooms. Maybe it was a decision they made after they left their room. I don't know. There a still a few questions about what happened, but Rachel is in no state of mind to deal with some of the details.' His captive audience nodded. 'Rachel was still in the wooded area when a man grabbed Mia. She was overpowered. I understand she put up a struggle. The murderer took a rock and began to smash it into her head.' Eleanor was not the only person with tears rolling down her cheeks. Grant's head was lowered, and his voice softened as he attempted to explain the circumstances.

The question came as a hush, 'What did Rachel do?'

'To my understanding, she was in shock, then the man looked around… and I can't even imagine the thoughts that went through her mind… in her mind, she thought it was me. In the dusk, he looked like me, and the jacket he was wearing was similar to … to the one I got last year at Gilmores.'

Almost in one breath, Eleanor and Mariah said,'Ian.'

'But at the time, Rachel did not know that. She… she did think it was me.' Daniela squeezed Grant's in reassurance that the nightmare was almost over. Taking a deep breath, Grant continued laying out the events. 'When I spoke to Rachel the previous day, all I knew was that she needed to be removed from where she was as soon as possible. As we know, Adrian has connections because of his work. This would not be the first person Adrian needed to locate who was in danger. He gave Fritz the necessary details of where Rachel was to be found. Once she was safe, then we could decide what to do. By then, Adrian had uncovered Henrik's blackmail role. At that time, we were not quite sure about the extent of Tiffany's and Ian's actual plan except the blackmailing.' Grant stopped talking and looked at Sylvia. 'I can't handle this cold coffee anymore. Can I have a fresh cup?'

Sylvia asked, 'Does anyone want anything else?'

Daniela stood up, 'I'll help.' Addressing Grant, she said, 'Don't wait for us. We know what happens.'

As they left the room with the dirty dishware, Grant continued, 'Fritz arrived minutes after Mia had been murdered. Rachel was shaking and couldn't speak. As Fritz approached her, she passed out… Shock? Fright? A combination? He was able to get her away to a safe house near Prague.' Looking down as he shook his head, he said slowly, 'She didn't want any part of me when I got there. She thought she saw me murder her friend.'

'When the police were looking for Mia, it was Rachel.'

'Kind of. I did stay away from Rachel for nearly twenty-four hours. Adrian was pulling in every favor he could. He had an acquaintance with Interpol.'

'Officer Svoboda?'

'No. Officer Svoboda's supervisor. When the Czech police found out that the DNA was very similar to mine and thread from the jacket that was most likely purchased from Gilmore, I knew I was on the top of the list as a suspect. Adrian and I decided it was time for me to get arrested in the States. We wanted to put as much distance between me and Rachel. At first, I didn't want to believe it, but certain items started to fall into place. The jacket was found thrown into a rubbish bin near the Charles River. We were lucky that someone didn't find it before us.'

Sylvia and Daniela returned to the library with fresh drinks. After sitting in silence for a moment to gather his thoughts, Grant continued the narrative, 'At that moment, the Czech Police thought that they had enough feasible circumstantial evidence to put me on trial. Until Adrian, Fritz, and I had a meeting with them. There were a couple of things that didn't make sense. The DNA they took from Mia's body was similar to mine but not identical. Also, why kill Mia Thyes?'

'Why?' Laura asked. 'What difference would it make if you were convicted or not? It wouldn't change your father's will.'

‘No, it would not. But there was another part to their plans. You know that Adrian was planning on retiring.’ Both sisters nodded, ‘Yes.’ ‘Of course, Eleanor, Mariah, mine, Ian, and Rachel are all part owners in the business. Our voting shares are 20% for me as CEO, the rest is 18%. Then, 4% is for the President of the Legal Division and 4% for the President of the Property Management Division. If Rachel's voting share is passed to Tiffany, and Henrik takes over a President, which is conceivable, the total voting block could be 40%.’

‘But even if this is true, there is 60% to keep them from making changes to the company. Correct?’ asked Mariah. Eleanor looked at her brother. ‘Grant, if you die or are incarcerated, who is your heir? Rachel?’

‘Actually, each of the nieces and nephews, including any future ones. But you are right. Rachel has my voting shares of the business.’

‘Wow!’ said Mariah. ‘So, if both you and Rachel are out of the picture, Tiffany, Ian, and Henrik share the spoils.’

‘Up to and including selling the business, which is why Dad structured the voting options the way he did.’

‘Why didn’t you tell the police -Czech – Interpol – Rochester Police-somebody about this in the beginning,’ demanded Mariah.

‘Because we had no proof or no idea what the final plan was or who to trust. Then there was Rachel, who would swear I murdered Mia. Anyway, Adrian and Fritz managed to convince the investigating police that there was more than a teenager’s death. But the priority was to keep Rachel safe. When the Thyes arrived in Prague, the Czech police and Fritz had the task of telling them their daughter wasn’t missing but dead. We need time to find evidence to prove theories.’ Grant looked around at his friends and family. ‘At the request of Interpol, the Czech police were able to keep the fact of incorrect identification concealed for a few days. When Mrs. Thyes went home, it was to allow Rachel to stay at the Thyes. But no one knew she was there. Fritz and his team smuggled her from Prague to Switzerland. I don’t know how the Thyes could handle having their daughter dead instead of Rachel. Mr. Thyes remained in Prague to continue with the missing Mia scheme. The authorities had convinced them that this was the best way of apprehending their daughter’s murderer once they realized it wasn’t me. We are so grateful to the Thyes. Between the Czech Police Force, Office Svoboda, and Fritz Munitz's team, once part of the plan was proven, other parts began to fall into place.'

Grant stood up, stretched, and walked to the wall, facing the thirty-five year old painting of himself, his parents, and his siblings. He was ten years old at the time, Eleanor and Mariah were eight and five, and Ian was barely two years old.. Then he turned his back on the picture and continued with the story. 'As you all know, I needed to come back to the States. I knew a warrant would be issued for my arrest. We needed to give the law enforcement time to investigate the theories we proposed.' Grant walked back to the sofa and sat on the arm next to Daniela. 'The major question was who was the investigator Henrik hired? Once he was identified, and a little checking into his financials and other activities, we had the entire plan.'

Laura's Oliver interrupted with a question. 'How did they think they could get away with it?'

'Millions of dollars can make anything seem possible. I was blocking Ian's fantasy, and Rachel was blocking Tiffany's. Henrik thought he got what he wanted, which was to both marry Tiffany and get a controlling interest in Priestly. We are not sure of the entire plan, but ultimately, the plan was to sell Priestly Enterprises. Since Dad's death, I have received several offers which, of course, I did not take seriously. But Henrik knew about them.'

'What happened today?' asked Eleanor.

He put his arms around Daniela and squeezed her. 'This is where Dani comes in. At the time it was happening, I was not happy, but now I am so grateful.'

'Stop messing with us, what do you mean?'

'Well, Dani did not want us to be seen in public.'

Facing Daniela, Eleanor asked why. 'Because I am horrendous ugly.' Grant responded.

Dani blushed as she poked Grant with her elbow, then she responded, 'No. I wasn't sure if our relationship would go the distance. Only Sylvia, Alex, and Rachel knew about us.'

Picking up her hand, Grant kissed it before he continued with the story. 'We didn't want to do anything to spook Ian, Tiffany, and Henrik while we were putting the pieces together. The most recent piece fell in place two days ago when Officer Claycross was arrested and flipped on Henrik who was also then arrested. Ex-officer Claycross would rather be charged with bribery than murder. It was time to have Rachel come home. We were sure Tiffany and Ian would be alibis for each other. Since everyone else in the family and other key friends like Laura was under suspicion, Dani was the only person to go to Rachel and bring her home, who was not under surveillance. The next part of the plan Sylvia and Alex put together.'

First Sylvia, then Alex, explained how they got Dani away from the eyes of the reporters and out of the country to England.

'England??? But Rachel was in Switzerland?'

Laura interrupted. 'I flew to England to be with Oliver and his parents a few days ago since his father had a relapse.' She added hurriedly, 'which he didn't. Then Oliver, Dani, and I took a tourist junket to Switzerland. We met up with Rachel. Grant is right. Rachel was … is… pretty much in shock over everything. She thought she saw Grant murder Mia. Whereas everything that was happening hadn't sunk in yet, Rachel now knows that it was a repulsive plan that Grant had no part in. She agreed to come back to Rochester. Oliver and I took an earlier flight home. Office Svoboda was on the same flight as Rachel just to ensure she would be all right. Also, to present the evidence at today's hearing.'

The story returned to Grant, 'We had made arrangements for Dani and Rachel to stay at Roselyn's house until this morning.' There was a pause. The story was almost over.

Sylvia asked, 'What is happening to Tiffany and Ian?'

'According to Adrian, they are throwing each other under the bus – multiple times. Becca was convinced that she was also involved and could be convicted of conspiracy to commit murder. She has confirmed several important details.'

The question hung in the air. Finally, Mariah asked, 'What about Rachel?

Roughly, Grant responded, 'She is going to live with me and Dani. And we try to get some type of balance back in her life after she has found out that her mother and her brother tried to murder her!'

Dani stood up and put her around the man she loved and who was hurting so much on behalf of his youngest sister. Sylvia also stood up. She and Alex began to gather the dishware. Laura said to Grant, 'Grant, we are going to head home. It has been a hell of a last month.'

Grant's moment of weakness passed. Rising from the arm of the sofa, he took Laura's hand in his. 'I cannot tell you… and Oliver… how much I appreciate your help during all this.'

Kissing her boss on the cheek, she said, 'I had to. We couldn't have a jailbird at our wedding.' After Laura and Oliver hugged Dani, they left the library.

Daniela looked at Grant, Eleanor, and Mariah, 'Darling, I need a hot shower. Eleanor and Mariah, I am so glad to finally meet you both.'

Exiting from the library, Daniela found Sylvia waiting for her, she said formally. 'Miss Dani, your clothes have been moved into Mr Grant's room.'

'Sylvia, that is not necessary.'

Smiling at the newest member of the household, 'Yes, it is.'

# Chapter 34

Santa Claus' grotto couldn't have any more seasonal cheer than the Priestly house a week before Christmas. Rochester weather also cooperated with six inches of snow that dropped the day before and the temperature remaining cold enough to make the street look like a fairyland.

As Rachel rushed past Daniela holding on to her new boyfriend, she stopped the teenager and said softly to her, 'Sweetie, you are missing one of your earrings.'

Rachel's hands flew to her earlobes, 'Oh no, it must have fallen off while we were dancing.' She grabbed what's-his-name hand, and they re-entered the heated gazebo attached to the conservatory where the dining area had now been converted into a dance floor. Holding her half-empty wine glass, she chatted to guests as her eyes searched for her husband. Dani couldn't help smiling when she thought about her marriage with Grant.

Just as Judge Wilkinson suggested, they were married by the registrar two days later. Eleanor, Mariah, Rachel, Daniela's mother, Clare, and her two sisters attended the ceremony. The conversation with her family the day before the ceremony was not pleasant. Her mother kept asking why she was getting married so quickly. Was she pregnant?

Since then, her mother kept referring to Daniela as her favorite daughter. Every day, Clare found an excuse to visit the house on Oakfield Street. Daniela was ready to have a few unpleasant words with her mother until a positive aspect emerged. Since Daniela was caring for Grandma Lucy until a carer/companion could be hired, her mother accompanied her on several visits. And behold! Her mother and Grandma Lucy became friends. Daniela made a slight suggestion that it would be extremely helpful if her mother could move from her one-bedroom apartment into Grandma Lucy's huge luxurious house temporarily. Clare jumped at the chance. As Clare told all her friends, it was the least she could do to help her poor daughter.

Daniela gave a slight wave to Eleanor and her family, talking to the obviously pregnant Laura. When Laura told her about the pregnancy, she laughed. 'I was so worried about one of my bridesmaids getting preggo. I never thought it would be me. At least this will be one incentive to lose the baby weight to fit into my wedding gown.'

A tap on her shoulder made her turn around, 'Cindy!' She placed her glass on a nearby table before wrapping her arms around her best friend. 'Did you just get here?'

'Yes, Allan's school pageant ran a little late. Tony and the kids are looking for the leftover food.'

'There are tons of it. They won't starve.' Grabbing her friend's hand, she headed toward the stairs. Once in her bedroom, the closed door to muffle the party sounds. Looking around the room, Cindy remarked, 'This room is bigger than my first apartment.' Laughing, Dani and Cindy sat in the two armchairs in front of the fireplace. 'So, how is Rachel doing?'

'I'm glad we decided to keep her here. Her grades are up and down, but we are not too worried about that. Grant says that they should be closing on Tiffany's house. The money will be put in a trust for her.' Daniela paused for a moment. 'Rachel is still having nightmares, but they are not as bad as they used to be.'

'Is she still going to therapy?'

'Definitely. Especially now….'

'I know, I saw the news. Tiffany and Ian are being expedited to the Czech Republic in January.'

'The worst part is that Rach has to go over there. Grant is researching if we can get her testimony over a video link.'

Their conversation was interrupted by a tap on the door. Grant opened the door slightly and asked, 'Can I come in?'

'Darling, of course. How did you know I was here? Oh, Thank you!' Grant handed each one of the ladies' champagnes in their wedding gift of Swarovski Crystal Champagne Flutes from Rowes which was presented when Daniela left her employment. Ken became overly enthusiastic and happy for her as he gave her the gift on behalf of the employees. Brian just scowled.

'I saw Tony and figured that you had kidnapped Cindy.' He sat on the small table between the armchairs. 'How was the recital?'

Laughing, she said, 'I had to nudge Tony awake twice. He said recitals are the worst part about being a stepfather.'

Standing up and kissing his wife, he said, 'Sweetie, I know once you two start talking, it will go on all night. Grandma Lucy and your mother are beginning to think that it is time to leave. I will hold everyone off for fifteen minutes. Then, it will be showtime again.'

'I promise I will be downstairs in fifteen minutes.' As he walked to the door, she added, 'I love you.'

Winking, Grant responded, 'I love you too.'

After the door closed, Cindy began the conversation again. 'Who would have ever thought two years ago – not only would you be with just one man - but married!'

Laughing, Dani responded, 'Forget marriage. I never thought I would meet a man I love as much as Grant.' Glazing into her champagne flute, then up at her friend. 'Cindy, the other day I was helping Rachel with her homework. Her assignment was a paper on JFK and what was his 'Camelot' plan for the United States. We found a quote he gave during his 1963 Berlin speech, in which he said, '*Change is the law of life. And those who look only to the past or present are certain to miss the future.*' I think that quote will become one of my favorite mottos.'

Acknowledgements

If I listed all the people who supported my writing dreams, the list would be longer than the novel itself. However, I will attempt to keep my Appreciation short.

I am grateful to my children and my children-in-law: Chris, Devin, John, Kelly, and Robin. When I began my novice attempts at storytelling, I knew I would receive straightforward opinions from them. And they delivered!

Much love to my most awesome grandchildren Abby, Brenden, John, Kalob, Kiera, and Kyler.

Thanks for the support from my sisters and parents especially my sister, Beverly, who read all my earliest stories.

And thank you to so many friends, male and female, who had faith in me when I didn't have faith in myself.

With the support from the people in my life, they have created a writing monster. Now so many people can see the smoke rising from the keyboard as my suppressed stories are tumbling into existence.

Thank You, Everyone!!!

Printed in Great Britain
by Amazon

36502927R00108